FOR EVERY WOMAN OVER 30—

*Have you had your ovaries removed?

*Are you thin? Are you petite?

*Do you have a fair complexion?

*Has you mother, aunt, or grandmother lost height?
Broken her hip?

*Are you a compulsive dieter?

*Do you hardly ever exercise?

*Have you never been pregnant?

*Do you stay away from birth control pills?

*Is your diet heavy in protein?

*Do you take antacids?

*Do you have "see-through" skin?

*Are you a smoker?

*Do you avoid milk and other dairy products?

*Do you have periodontal disease?

*Do you suffer from excessive stress?

IF YOU'VE ANSWERED "YES" TO EVEN
A FEW OF THESE QUESTIONS,
YOU MAY BE HEADED TOWARD CHRONIC DISABILITY
FOR THE LAST THIRD OF YOUR LIFE.

STAND TALL!
Every Woman's Guide to Preventing Osteoporosis

STAND TALL!

Every Woman's Guide to Preventing Osteoporosis

By Morris Notelovitz, M.D., Ph.D.
and Marsha Ware

Illustrations by Jeff Erickson

BANTAM BOOKS
TORONTO • NEW YORK • LONDON • SYDNEY • AUCKLAND

STAND TALL!
EVERY WOMAN'S GUIDE TO PREVENTING OSTEOPOROSIS

*A Bantam Book / published by arrangement with
Triad Publishing Co., Inc.*

PRINTING HISTORY

*Triad edition published November 1982
3 printings through January 1984*

*A Selection of Prevention Book Club (Rodale Press), July 1983
and Nurses Book Club (Jason Aaronson).*

Related articles or excerpts appeared in PREVENTION, *February
1983;* VOGUE, *May 1983;* THE NEW YORK TIMES, *January 1984;* YOUR
GOOD HEALTH, *February 1984;* FAMILY CIRCLE, *March 1984;*
SHAPE, *July 1984;* HEALTH, *August 1984;* GLAMOUR, *September
1984;* NEWSWEEK, *September 1984; and* CONSUMER REPORTS,
October 1984.

Bantam edition / April 1985

Library of Congress Cataloging in Publication Data

Notelovitz, Morris.
Stand tall!

Reprint. Originally published: Gainesville, Fla.:
Triad Pub. Co., © 1982.

Bibliography: p. 169
Includes index.
1. Osteoporosis—Prevention 2. Women—Health and hygiene.
I. Ware, Marsha. II. Title.
RC931.0'73N67 1985   616.7'1   84-24338
ISBN 0-553-34143-X (pbk.)

Published simultaneously in the United States and Canada

PRINTED IN THE UNITED STATES OF AMERICA

DC   0 9 8 7 6 5 4 3 2

To climacteric well-being.   — M.N.

To my parents, for their gift of education.   — M.W.

We wish to thank the staff and faculty of the Center for Climacteric Studies for their help and cooperation, the clients of the Osteoporosis Screening Program for allowing us use of their records, and the women who graciously shared with us and with you their feelings and experiences. Special thanks go to Paul Mullins for his otherwise thankless task of retrieving books from the library.

Contents

Illustrations

Graphs

Charts

Foreword

Osteoporosis has often been called a "silent disease." Technically this is because it produces absolutely no symptoms until a fracture occurs. There is, however, another sense in which the disorder is silent, perhaps even invisible. Despite the fact that osteoporosis is an extremely common problem (as the authors point out, it is more prevalent than diabetes in postmenopausal women), it is largely unknown to the general public, particularly to federal policymakers. The authors of *Stand Tall!* attempt to rectify this situation, to overcome the invisibility — the silence — of osteoporosis.

Unlike many other popular books in the field of health, *Stand Tall!* is a serious effort to provide essential information to the concerned and intelligent layperson. It offers help, but it is not just another self-help book. It provides relevant common sense information about diet, but it does not promote a miracle diet or cure. The authors explain in largely nontechnical language what the scientific community now understands about osteoporosis. The roles of hormones, diet, and exercise in causing, preventing, and treating this common disorder are discussed, and explanations of the various tests used in relation to osteoporosis are given.

This book goes a long way toward telling patients with osteoporosis, their families, and those who may develop the disorder both what we know and what we don't know about the problem. It helps to close the gap of unequal knowledge between physician and lay person.

Although much remains to be learned, research has advanced to a point where we are now able to ask a number of critical questions, the answers to which could lead to a significant reduction of the incidence of osteoporosis. It is important, therefore, that sufficient public attention be addressed to this issue to ensure that the requisite funding is available to carry

out the targeted research. Better public awareness of osteoporosis and better understanding of its character are necessary
steps to that end.

Robert P. Heany, MD
Creighton University
Omaha, Nebraska

Preface

This book was written in response to an urgent need for practical information on osteoporosis and its prevention. More common in older women than heart attacks, strokes, diabetes, rheumatoid arthritis, or breast cancer, osteoporosis presents one of the greatest health threats to your later years both in terms of the quality and the length of your life.

Long accepted as a natural part of aging, this potentially crippling condition is just beginning to receive the attention it deserves. In *Stand Tall!* we have included the most up-to-date information from worldwide research. Wherever possible, we have translated the scientific data into meaningful suggestions you can use for your own program of prevention. Our goal is to help you understand everything that is currently known about osteoporosis and how it can affect your health, so you can make educated decisions.

Designing an individualized program of prevention involves decisions to be made *together by an informed woman and her physician.* Unfortunately, with only newspapers or magazines to rely on for your health information, becoming an informed woman is not easy. These sources are sometimes slow in reporting medical news and their articles are frequently brief and incomplete.

The information you need is here in *Stand Tall!* Read it, think about it, and go to your physician with questions. Discuss your chances of developing osteoporosis and the best way to go about preventing it. As a woman, you can expect to live one-third of your life after menopause. Become an informed health-care consumer, and take an active role in making these years healthy ones!

Morris Notelovitz
Marsha Ware
October, 1982

Why Osteoporosis Should Concern You

Osteoporosis is not a disease per se, but rather it is the end result of severe or prolonged bone loss. By bone loss we mean the gradual thinning and increased porosity of bones (hence the name osteoporosis) that occurs naturally with aging but which can be dangerously accelerated or beneficially slowed down by a multitude of factors.

Osteoporosis is a painful, disfiguring, and debilitating process. As the bones thin and weaken, they become less able to withstand the physical stresses of everyday living. The stereotype of the "little old lady" refers to the older woman whose bone loss has progressed to the point where she has lost several inches of height due to painful collapsing of the spine. Such a woman has the classic "dowager's hump," recurring back pain and, frequently, fractures of her wrist and hip.

Osteoporosis is a women's issue. Loss of bone begins sooner and proceeds twice as rapidly in women as it does in men. Osteoporosis affects 25 percent of women after a natural menopause. Of those who have undergone a surgical menopause (removal of the ovaries) without hormone replacement therapy, up to 50 percent will develop osteoporosis.

Osteoporosis cannot be cured, but it can be prevented. Prevention strategies are simple: proper nutrition, adequate exercise and, for some women, hormone replacement therapy. To be most effective, these measures must be undertaken before bone loss begins and be continued for life. At present there are no acceptable treatments that can restore bone once it is lost. By beginning early, you *can* prevent osteoporosis.

1

Your Bones and How They Change

Your skeleton consists of 206 bones, and they are all you are going to have. How you take care of them will determine how long they last and how well they do the job they were meant to do. Your bones offer support and protection to your body while enabling you to move around. At the same time, they manufacture blood cells and store 99 percent of your body's calcium.

Unless you happen to break one, you probably do not give your bones much thought. If you have not specifically studied the subject, you might be surprised to learn that bones are not solid and lifeless, but are actually living tissues richly supplied with blood vessels, nerve fibers, and fluid-filled channels. They are among the most complex tissues in your body, and it is not an exaggeration to say that almost everything that happens to you also has an affect on them. Throughout your life, your

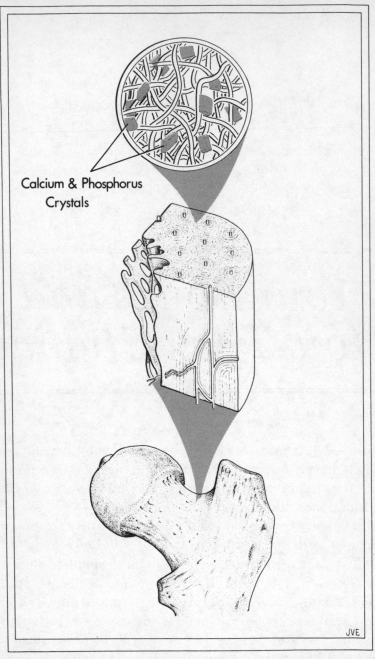

Calcium & Phosphorus
Crystals

JVE

WHAT ARE BONES MADE OF? The structure of bone at the microscopic level (top), in cross-section (center), and as it appears to the naked eye (bottom).

bones will be affected by heredity, diet, hormones, physical activity, stress, injury, disease, and drugs.

Bone Remodeling

Like all living tissue, bone is constantly being broken down and re-formed; this cyclic process is called *bone remodeling*. What actually happens is that small quantities of bone are lost through breakdown (resorption) on the inner surface (the surface lining the bone marrow cavity), while at the same time new bone tissue is formed on the outer surface. The same remodeling process occurs on the microscopic surfaces throughout the bone. The net result is that your bones get bigger and denser (but not so heavy that you can't carry them around). Your *bone mass* — the total amount of bone in your skeleton — is maintained by a delicate balance of these two processes. This balance changes constantly in response to the needs of your body.

WHAT ARE BONES MADE OF?

Bone tissue is composed of tiny crystals of calcium and phosphorus embedded in a framework of interlocking protein fibers. These protein fibers are made primarily of collagen. It is the calcium crystals that give your bones their strength, hardness, and rigidity, and the collagen fibers that give them their relative capacity for flexibility. A number of other materials are also present in bone — fluoride, sodium, potassium, magnesium, citrate — as well as a host of trace elements. These act as the "mortar" holding the "bricks" of calcium and phosphorus crystals together.

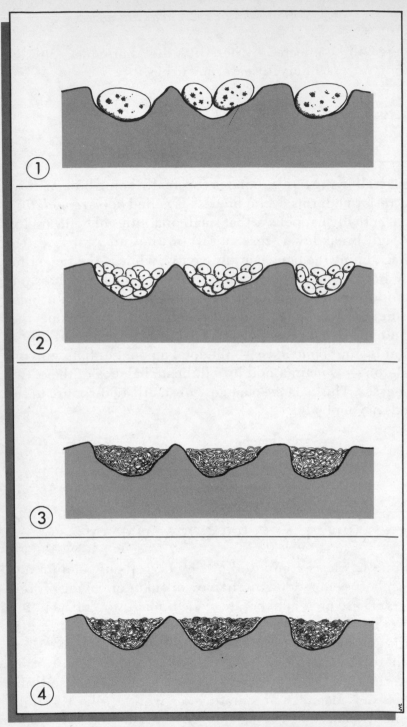

FOUR-STEP SEQUENCE OF NEW BONE FORMATION

All Bones Are Not Created Equal

Although all bones undergo age-related changes, all are not affected in exactly the same way. The differences are due to the structural makeup of the two basic kinds of bone tissue.

The first is *cortical bone,* which looks solid and dense. The second type is *trabecular bone,* which is more porous and looks much like a honeycomb. Every bone is composed of both types, with the trabecular inside, surrounded by the cortical. The relative proportions of each differ from one bone to another and even within parts of an individual bone. The vertebrae of your spine, for example, are mostly the porous trabecular bone surrounded by a thin cortical shell. At the other extreme are the

HOW NEW BONE IS MADE

New bone formation is required for growth, for repair of the microscopic fractures resulting from everyday physical stress, and for the replacement of worn-out bone. It is dependent upon a four-step bone remodeling cycle.

1. The cycle begins with a small amount of bone breakdown. The *osteoclasts,* the bone-resorbing (bone-breakdown) cells, dig microscopic cavities along the inner surfaces of the bone.

2. Next, the *osteoblasts,* the bone-forming cells, fill in the cavities with new bone cells. Many osteoblasts are required to replace the bone removed by one osteoclast.

3. Once the osteoblasts are in place, they produce the collagen matrix of the new bone.

4. Approximately 10 days later, the calcium and phosphorus crystals are laid down in the framework. This process is called *bone mineralization* and takes several weeks to months to complete.

The entire cycle lasts approximately 3 to 4 months. It is estimated that adults have 10 to 30 percent of their bone replaced each year through this process.

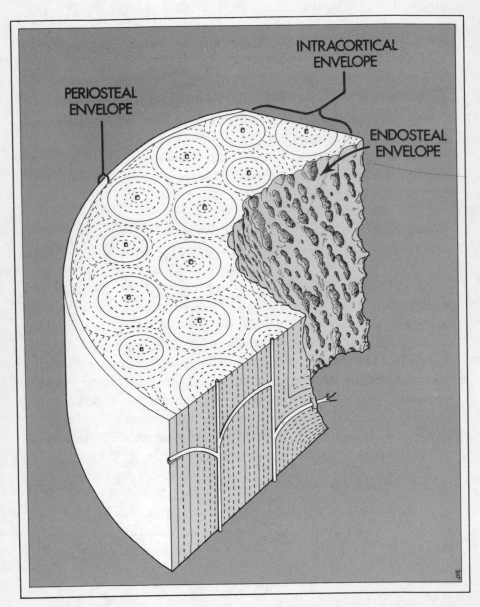

PERIOSTEAL
ENVELOPE

INTRACORTICAL
ENVELOPE

ENDOSTEAL
ENVELOPE

CROSS-SECTION OF BONE.

hard, long bones of your arms and legs, which are mostly cortical bone with areas of trabecular bone concentrated at both ends.

Despite its delicate appearance, trabecular bone is actually very strong — its latticework structure provides maximum support with a minimum of material. But all those fine surfaces create an enormous amount of exposed area, and so more bone loss can occur there. For this reason, those bones or parts of bones that are richest in trabecular tissue are the most vulnerable to disturbances in the bone remodeling process.

How Your Age Affects Your Bones

The human body changes as it ages, and the skeleton is no exception. In the early part of life, as a child grows, the changes are very visible; later changes are less obvious, but occur nonetheless.

THE THREE FACES OF BONE

Bone has three surfaces, called *envelopes*. Each envelope has different anatomical features, even though its cell makeup is identical to the other two. The surface facing the marrow cavity is known as the *endosteal envelope*, the outer surface is the *periosteal envelope*, while the material in between is called the *intracortical envelope*.

Throughout childhood, new bone formation occurs on the (outer) periosteal envelope, and a lesser amount of breakdown occurs on the (inner) endosteal envelope. During adolescence, bone formation occurs on both surfaces, leading to large overall gains in bone mass. During early adulthood, bone breakdown begins again on the endosteal (inner) envelope, heralding the beginning of the age-related decline in bone mass.

In contrast to the bone loss of aging, which occurs on the endosteal surface, bone loss associated with immobilization or prolonged bed rest takes place in the intracortical envelope.

From the time you are born until you reach early adulthood, you produce more new bone tissue than you lose through bone breakdown. Children's skeletons enlarge because the amount of new tissue formed on the outer surfaces of their bones exceeds that which is broken down on the inner surfaces.

Adolescence brings about an acceleration in growth that is related to the surge in sex hormone production. Estrogens and progesterone in girls, and androgens in boys, stimulate the formation of new bone on the outer surface. Later in adolescence, more bone is added on the inner surface and in the intracortical envelope. The tremendous growth spurts that adolescents have are due to the laying down of new bone tissue on *both* the inner and outer surfaces of existing bone.

Although it eventually slows somewhat, this is the pattern of growth that continues into adulthood. Then the childhood pattern of bone remodeling resumes, with outer surface formation and inner surface breakdown. Now, however, the rate of breakdown exceeds that of new formation, and bone mass begins to decline.

How Are Women and Men Different?

Both women and men lose bone as they get older; the difference is in the amount and in the rate of loss. Unbelievable as it seems, decline of bone mass begins — for both sexes — in the early 20s with the loss of trabecular bone from the spine. From the start, women lose bone much more rapidly than men do. By the time she reaches 80, a woman will have lost 47 percent of her trabecular bone — almost half! — and a man only 14 percent.

Cortical bone mass reaches its peak around age 30 to 35; from then until about 50, both sexes experience a slight loss, primarily from the long bones of the arms and legs. But then a woman — if she has experienced menopause — will begin losing cortical bone *twice as fast* as a man does.

Women lose bone most rapidly in the first 5 to 6 years following menopause. Their loss at this time is actually six times as rapid as a man's. A new pattern of bone remodeling then emerges that is the mirror image of the growth spurt that followed the adolescent hormone surges. In fact, if a woman does nothing to prevent it, it is estimated that by age 55 the bone lost may be equivalent to that gained during her adolescent growth phase.

Around the age of 65, a woman's rate of bone loss begins to slow down, again becoming similar to that of men. But keep in mind that even though the *rate* of loss slows, women have already lost a great deal more bone than men at this point. Both women and men then continue to slowly, but steadily, lose bone as a natural part of the aging process.

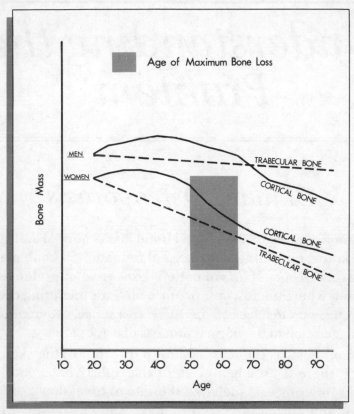

BONE LOSS WITH AGE: A COMPARISON OF MEN AND WOMEN.

2

Understanding the Problem

Defining Osteoporosis

A certain amount of age-related bone loss is normal and, as far as we know, inevitable. This normal reduction in bone mass is called *osteopenia*. If loss of bone is excessive or prolonged to the point where microscopic or more obvious fracturing occurs, a person is said to have *osteoporosis*. In a sense, osteoporosis is an exaggeration of the normal process of osteopenia.

Osteoporosis is the most common disorder of the skeleton. With it there is an uncoupling of the tightly balanced bone remodeling process, such that the rate of breakdown exceeds that of new formation. Studies have shown that new bone formation is essentially normal, but the rate of breakdown is increased. If nothing is done to prevent it, excessive amounts of bone tissue can be lost, resulting in a great reduction of the actual bone mass.

Osteoporosis affects both the amount and strength of bone tissue. The porous trabecular bone succumbs first and becomes even more porous. Later, as bone continues to erode, cortical bone is affected as well, becoming thinner. Thin porous bones are weak bones, and weak bones are easily fractured. Fractures result when the bones are no longer strong enough to withstand the physical stresses of everyday activity.

Types of Osteoporosis. Scientists usually separate osteoporosis into two types — *primary* and *secondary*. Secondary osteoporosis can often be attributed to a single cause, usually some drug or disease, and can occur in men as well as women and in children as well as adults. The more common, primary osteoporosis, on the other hand, usually results from a complex interplay of many factors, of which heredity, hormones, and nutrition are probably the most influential. Primary osteoporosis is sometimes called *postmenopausal osteoporosis* because it occurs most commonly in older women. (Recent research indicates that within each type there may be a further division into *trabecular* and *cortical osteoporosis,* depending on which kind of bone is more severely affected. So far it is not known whether these really are two separate problems with different causes and means of prevention.)

Osteoporotic bone differs in no way from normal bone; there is just less of it. This makes osteoporosis different from other bone diseases, most of which are associated with abnormal bone composition. With *osteomalacia,* for example, the adult equivalent of rickets, there is a deficiency of calcium and phosphorus crystals in the collagen framework of bone. Usually caused by a vitamin D deficiency, this disorder is more

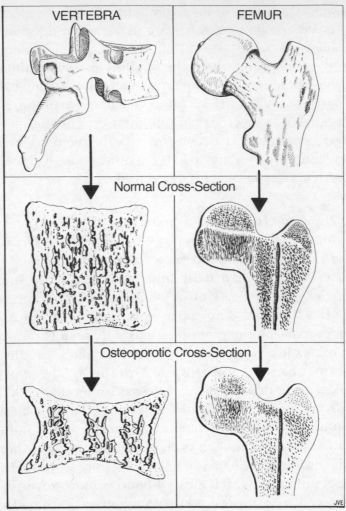

| VERTEBRA | FEMUR |

Normal Cross-Section

Osteoporotic Cross-Section

HOW OSTEOPOROSIS AFFECTS BONE. Because they contain large proportions of the honeycomb-like trabecular bone, the spinal vertebrae and upper part of the femur (thigh bone) are especially vulnerable to disturbances of the bone remodeling process. Trabecular bone makes up 90% of the body of the vertebrae. As osteoporosis progresses, much of this trabecular bone is lost and the thin cortical shell is no longer able to support the weight it normally bears, and it collapses. The upper part of the femur contains both cortical and trabecular bone. At its weakest point, the neck, which joins the round tip to the long, heavy shaft of the bone, there is 50% trabecular and 50% cortical bone. With osteoporosis, the trabecular bone becomes more porous and the outer cortical shell becomes thinner.

common in areas with limited sunshine, because sun exposure stimulates production of vitamin D in the body.

Osteomalacia is sometimes found together with osteoporosis; about 25 percent of Northern European women who sustain hip fractures due to osteoporosis also have osteomalacia. In this country, however, the figure is less than 10 percent because we have more direct sunlight and greater fortification of our foods with vitamin D.

While the causes and mechanisms of osteoporosis are complex and varied, the end result is always the same — fragile bones that are easily fractured.

What Can Happen
If You Have Osteoporosis

Fractures of the Spinal Vertebrae

Because the bones of the spine — the vertebrae — are primarily composed of the meshlike trabecular bone, they are usually the first to show the signs and effects of osteoporosis. As the years of losing bone take their toll, and the vertebrae become more porous and weak, they go through various stages of structural deformity. In time, they can actually collapse.

Vertebral fractures can occur spontaneously, with the weakened bones simply collapsing under the weight of the body. More commonly, however, they follow sudden attempts to extend the spine from a flexed position. This can happen as a result of such everyday activities as opening a window, lifting a child, or making a bed.

If several vertebrae collapse (and this is often the case), five may fill the space normally occupied by three. Continued fractures can result in the rib cage tilting downward toward the hips, eventually coming to rest on the hipbones. The outcome is outward curvature of the upper spine (kyphosis), leading to the dowager's hump; inward curvature of the lower spine (lordosis); and a protruding abdomen, because the downward movement of the ribs forces the internal organs outward. The accompanying pain is almost always severe.

The physical deformities that accompany vertebral fractures result in varying degrees of disability. The loss of height usually occurs in stepwise bursts of 1 inch or more, corresponding to the collapse of one or more vertebrae. It is not unusual for a woman with osteoporosis to lose as much as 2 inches of height in a period of just a few weeks. Eventually she may lose a total of 8 inches or more from her adult height, all from the upper part of her body. There is no change in the length of the long bones of the arms and legs. Needless to say, these fractures and the resultant deformities and disability are accompanied by a great deal of emotional pain.

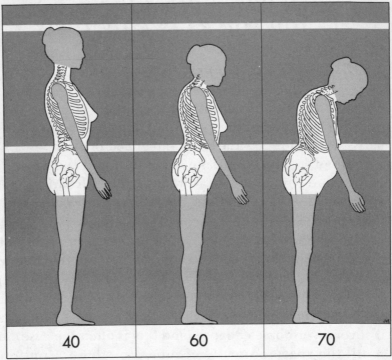

40   60   70

THE SHRINKING WOMAN. Spinal vertebrae weakened by osteoporosis collapse causing loss of height (all from the upper part of the body), inward curvature of the lower spine, outward curvature of the upper spine, and protruding of the abdomen.

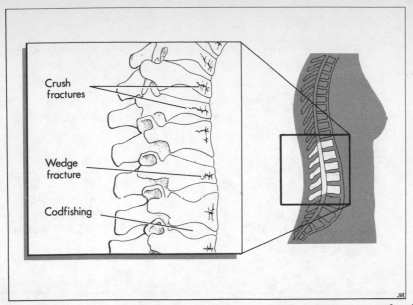

TYPES OF VERTEBRAL FRACTURES. Most vertebral fractures occur in the middle region of the back. They can be classified in terms of increasing degree of severity: "codfishing," wedge fractures, and crush fractures.

STAGES OF VERTEBRAL COLLAPSE

In the first stages of bone collapse, the affected vertebrae take on a biconcave shape in a vain attempt to maintain the structural integrity of the spine and to support the weight of the body. When two adjacent vertebrae are so affected, the space between them becomes fish-shaped; "codfishing" is the word used to describe this condition. Eventually the strain is too much, and the anterior side (toward the front of the body) of the bone collapses, producing what doctors call the characteristic "wedge fracture," which is easily recognized on spinal X-rays. As the process continues, the posterior side (toward the back of the body) may collapse as well. The result at that point is a compact and totally collapsed vertebra (a "crush" fracture). Wedged and crushed vertebrae occur most often in the region of the middle of the back, at the junction of the thoracic and lumbar vertebrae, because these are the vertebrae that bear most of the weight.

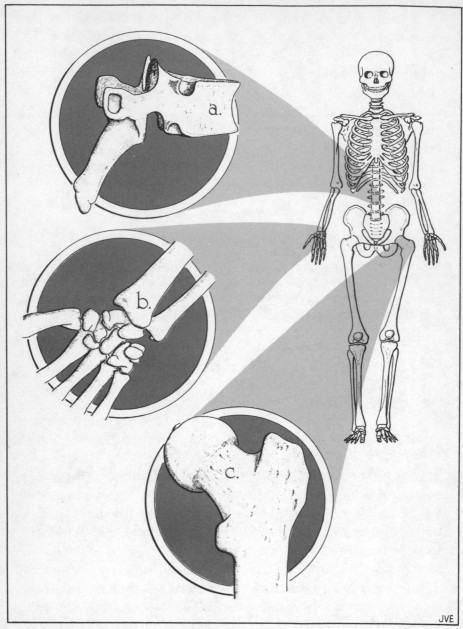

THREE PRINCIPAL SITES OF OSTEOPOROTIC FRACTURES. Fractures of the spinal vertebrae, the wrist, and the hip are the most commonly associated with osteoporosis, although other types of fractures are not unusual.

Vertebral fractures are most likely to occur between the ages of 50 and 70, with the average age about 60. Half of all 65-year-old women have detectable wedging of one or more of their vertebrae, and 10 percent have at least one totally collapsed vertebra.

After having one or more vertebral fractures, a woman's risk of a second series of fractures is the same as before, depending in each case on the degree of osteoporosis and her exposure to trauma or physical stress.

The Pain of Spinal Fractures. The pain associated with vertebral (spinal) fractures typically follows a two-phase pattern. In the *acute phase*, there is intense pain localized at the site of the fracture. The pain is due not only to the fracture itself, but also to damage done to surrounding tissues. There may also be accompanying muscle spasm. This stage usually lasts from 1 to 4 weeks, until the bone heals itself in the new, collapsed form.

The *chronic phase* follows the acute phase and can last from 6 months to a year. The pain felt during this period is a less severe mid or lower backache and is largely due to muscle spasm and ligament strain. After the chronic phase has passed, a woman is said to be in *remission,* and she may have no pain or muscle spasms . . . until she fractures another vertebra.

Wrist Fractures

Wrist fractures usually happen when a woman has extended her arm to break a fall. Fractures incurred in this manner are sometimes called *Colle's fractures*. Although they usually heal easily and do not lead to any subsequent disability, they do serve as a warning that loss of cortical bone has occurred, and thus they may herald the more serious hip fracture.

The lower part of the radius (the shorter and thicker of the two forearm bones) contains about 25 percent trabecular and 75 percent cortical bone. A loss of both types thins and weakens the bone, accounting for the sharp rise in wrist fractures in women over the age of 50. At this age, such fractures are ten times more common in women than in men.

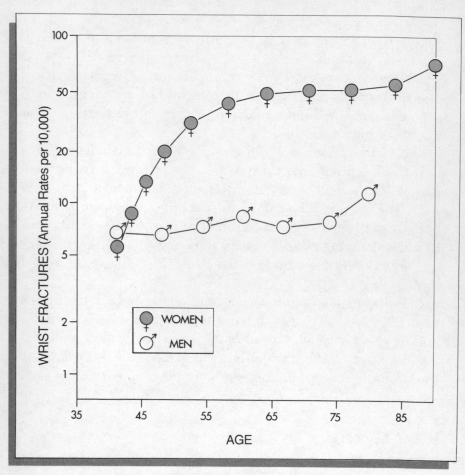

WRIST FRACTURES IN MEN AND WOMEN.

Hip Fractures

Hip fractures — more accurately, fractures of the upper part of the femur (the thigh bone) — are without a doubt the most disabling and life-threatening consequence of osteoporosis. Because of the relatively larger amount of hard cortical bone in the upper femur, it is the older woman with advanced osteoporosis who is the most likely to sustain a hip fracture.

(The loss of cortical bone is the precipitating factor in these fractures.)

Long ago it was thought that women were more susceptible to hip fractures because they were clumsy and tripped over their long skirts. We now know, of course, that women break their hips more often than men do because they have lost larger amounts of bone. Unlike vertebral fractures, which can occur spontaneously, hip fractures usually follow an injury. Though frequently caused by an accident such as falling in a bathtub or slipping on a rug, most of the time a fracture follows an injury that normal bones could easily withstand. Sometimes a hip fracture can occur with no apparent cause ... leading to the unanswerable question: Did she break her hip because she fell, or did she fall because she broke her hip?

The consequences of hip fracture can be devastating. Fewer than one-half of all women who suffer a hip fracture regain normal function. Fifteen percent die shortly after their injury, and nearly 30 percent die within 1 year. A recent study followed the progress of 108 hip fracture patients — 81 were women — for one year after their injury. After the initial hospital stay, 41 percent were transferred directly to a nursing home (the others returned home, went to another hospital, or had died). At the end of the year, 23 percent of these had been able to return home, 11 percent had died, and 66 percent remained in the nursing homes.

Deaths from hip fractures are not caused by the fracture itself but from some condition resulting from confinement to a hospital or nursing home bed, such as pneumonia, thrombosis (blood clots), or a fat embolism (bone marrow fat trapped in the lung).

One of the reasons hip fractures are so dangerous is that they frequently recur — persons suffering a break in the upper part of the femur are twenty times more likely to develop a hip fracture of the opposite side. It has been estimated that, on the average, a hip fracture reduces a woman's life expectancy by 12 percent. Thus, falls are the leading cause of accidental death in elderly white women in this country. (This is not the case for black women, who have a much lower incidence of hip fractures than white women.) Overall, hip fractures are the 12th leading cause of death in America today.

The Extent of the Problem

Every year 200,000 osteoporotic American women over the age of 45 fracture one or more of their bones. Of these, over 40,000 die of complications following their injuries. Many of the remainder lead significantly altered lives due to chronic pain and disability.

Right now there are 45 million women in the United States over the age of 40; they represent 20 percent of the total population and 38 percent of the female population. Older women are becoming the fastest growing segment of our

ANATOMY OF A HIP FRACTURE

A hip fracture is actually a fracture of the upper part of the thigh bone, the *femur*. Most fractures occur at the weakest part, the *neck*, although they can also occur in the *shaft* or *head* of the femur.

Hip fractures require immediate medical attention, and the patient is usually hospitalized for 3 to 6 weeks. Metal pins or screws are used to join the broken sections of the bone, and severe fractures may require replacement of the femoral head with a prosthetic (artificial) device. Recovery from a hip fracture depends on the severity of the fracture and the age and general state of health of the patient.

After a hip fracture, serious and even fatal complications can arise. If the femoral neck is severely fractured and fails to heal, the head of the femur can lose its blood supply and die. When this happens, the femoral head must be removed and replaced with an artificial one.

population, making osteoporosis a rapidly increasing problem. As these women enter the older age groups, their risk of fractures escalates.

Osteoporosis promises to become one of the most significant international health problems as well, as developing nations gain the medical technologies to extend the life expectancies of their citizens.

ONE FRACTURE CAN INCREASE THE RISK OF ANOTHER

A woman who has one type of osteoporotic fracture is much more likely to suffer another type of fracture than is a non-osteoporotic woman of the same age. In a study of hip fracture patients in Rochester, Minnesota, 18 percent had a history of a Colle's (wrist) fracture and 26 percent had X-ray evidence of vertebral fractures. Rib fractures had occurred in 17 percent of the patients.

In a study of British women with osteoporosis:

Those with *crush fractures* of the spine were four times as likely as non-osteoporotic women to also have wrist fractures and eight times as likely to have hip fractures.

Those with *hip fractures* were twice as likely to also have wrist fractures and six times as likely to have crush fractures of the spine.

Those with *wrist fractures* were four times as likely to have hip fractures and twice as likely to have crush fractures of the spine.

The results indicate the progressive nature of osteoporosis and the multiple disabilities it can produce.

The Monetary Cost

Osteoporosis is expensive. The average immediate cost for the first 9 days of hospitalization after a hip fracture is $10,000, and this does not include the cost of subsequent care and rehabilitation. In the United States alone, over $1 billion is spent each year for the care and treatment of older women with osteoporosis.

Recent statistics indicate that the number of women with hip fractures is increasing. This, coupled with inflation, leads experts to predict that by 1990, the annual national expense of osteoporosis will rise to over $3 billion.

The Emotional Cost

While osteoporosis presents a significant financial burden, hospitalization and therapy costs are only part of the problem. Should you become a victim of osteoporosis, the pain, deformity, and disability could profoundly affect your emotional well-being and life satisfaction.

The physical deformities caused by multiple vertebral fractures — the stooped posture, the dowager's hump, and the protruding abdomen — can viciously assault your self-image and esteem. You may feel less attractive and much older than your peers. You must face the fact that *never again* will you look the way you used to. The physical changes in shape and posture will make it difficult for you to find clothes that fit properly and attractively.

With the physical deformities can come disability and loss of independence. This is especially true in the case of a hip fracture. You may have to make adjustments in your life-style, often having to rely on family and friends to fulfill the simplest of needs. If you were an active, sociable woman, this may be the most difficult challenge to face.

Not one of the many studies on osteoporosis has focused on the psychosocial aspects of this common disorder. But research in other chronic and disabling diseases reveals that with the necessary adjustments in life-style can come stress, which is often disguised as anxiety, fear, guilt, depression, feelings of helplessness, or dread of the future.

Often a woman must face these challenges at a time when she is confronting other major life issues, such as divorce, widowhood (the average age of widowhood is only 56), retirement, or her husband's retirement. If she is married, her husband may have his own health problems and life crises as well.

THE OLD COURTESAN (*Rodin, 1855*)

Eve's Story

Five years ago Eve, who is now 67, experienced the first of a series of vertebral fractures that have caused her a great deal of pain. Spinal X-rays showed that she had at least two wedge fractures and eight crush fractures; her height has dropped from 5'7" to 4'11". Eve describes how this has affected her life and her attitudes about herself and those around her.

The first fracture happened when my husband and I were moving some furniture around the house. Because I was always strong and never hesitated to move things, I picked up a chair to take it into the garage. As I opened the door and put down the chair I heard something crack in my back. It was painful, but I thought I was all right. We even went to a party that night, even though a friend told me she could see the pain in my face.

The pain got progressively worse over the next couple of months. Any movement of my back, chest, or ribs was absolute agony — the pain was excruciating. I had trouble sleeping because even lying down hurt so badly. By this time I was nearly crippled. I couldn't bend or stoop. I couldn't even walk around. The pain would be so bad I'd cry sometimes.

After a while the pain started to subside and I could get around a little. My husband would ask me to come outside with him for a bit and that would make me feel better. Eventually I could go out shopping for a short time.

I didn't really want to go anywhere, though. People who knew me didn't recognize me. I didn't want to see anybody because of the way I looked.

One of the hardest things is finding clothes. I can't get into anything anymore. I can't dress and look like anybody because of the hump on my back. By the time I get something to fit around the hump and around my stomach, it's too big everywhere else. My legs are still long but I'm so short and wide on top. It's hard because I used to love clothes. My husband won't go shopping with me anymore because it hurts him so much to see me try to get clothes.

A problem most people wouldn't think of is going to a restaurant. The tables are too high. I feel like a little kid who needs a booster seat. I can practically push the food off my plate into my mouth. Now I take cushions with me to sit on and it's much better.

Sometimes I get very self-conscious and feel like everyone is looking at me. I don't like to be with people we used to know because they look at me and wonder what happened. I'd rather meet new people who can't compare me to what I used to look like.

I know now that what I have is osteoporosis and that it took many years for it to develop. But I didn't know then. It would be good for young women to find out about osteoporosis and for their doctors to be conscientious and tell them what they can do to prevent it.

3

How Your Body Regulates Bone Mass

Calcium and the "Bone Hormones"

Ninety-nine percent of your body's calcium is in your skeleton, so it is not surprising that calcium plays an important role in bone physiology. The importance of calcium to the body doesn't stop there, however. It is also essential for normal muscle contraction, blood clotting, and brain function.

Because calcium is so vital, the human body has evolved an elaborate system of hormones to ensure there is always enough of it in your blood. A regulating mechanism — a sort of "calcium thermostal" — controls calcium levels and bone mass. Three hormones are primarily involved: parathyroid hormone, vitamin D, and calcitonin.

Parathyroid Hormone

The parathyroids are four tiny glands in your neck at the base of the thyroid gland. If the calcium in your blood should fall below critical levels, these glands release *parathyroid hormone* into your bloodstream. The released hormone acts to increase the level of calcium in your blood.

1. It signals the kidneys to put calcium back into the bloodstream; this is calcium that would otherwise be excreted in the urine.

2. It stimulates the conversion of vitamin D from an inactive to an active form, which allows the intestines to absorb more calcium from the foods you eat.

3. It stimulates the breakdown of bone, which in turn releases stored calcium into the bloodstream.

Calcium is so critical to life, your body is willing to sacrifice bone mass to ensure adequate levels of it in your blood.

Vitamin D

Vitamin D is probably more correctly considered a hormone than a vitamin. It is available primarily from the sun (produced by the ultraviolet irradiation of an inactive form of vitamin D in your skin) and in limited amounts from foods such as eggs, milk, and fish.

Vitamin D is stored in the liver in a partially activated form and transported to the kidneys where it is converted into its final, activated state. Activated vitamin D has two calcium-conserving effects:

1. It increases the absorption of calcium in the intestines.

2. It increases the reabsorption of calcium through the kidneys.

Like parathyroid hormone, vitamin D is responsible for maintaining a proper level of calcium in the blood. But if the need for calcium is sufficiently great or if vitamin D is present in high levels, it can actually withdraw calcium from the bones, leading to bone loss.

In other words, the correct amount of vitamin D is beneficial — it helps to maintain a positive calcium balance — but an excess can have the reverse effect and cause you to lose bone unnecessarily.

Calcitonin

Calcitonin, a hormone released mainly by the thyroid gland, protects bones from the dissolving effects of parathyroid hormone and activated vitamin D. Because of its actions it is often referred to as a "calcium sparing" hormone. How it works is still not completely understood, but there is evidence to suggest that calcitonin directly inhibits the activity of the osteoclasts, the cells that break down bone.

We don't know as much about calcitonin as we do about parathyroid hormone or vitamin D, but we do know that men have more of it than women, and women with osteoporosis have less of it than women with normal amounts of bone. Calcitonin levels decrease with age, which is another reason we all lose bone as we get older.

Bone Loss At Menopause

For many years, scientists have been aware of a close association between the beginning of menopause and accelerated bone loss. It has made no difference whether the menopause was natural or surgical: a 45-year-old woman whose ovaries have been removed at 35 will have as little bone mass as a 60-year-old woman who has a natural menopause at 50. (In contrast, women still menstruating in their 50s maintain normal bone mass until they stop menstruating; then they begin the typical pattern of postmenopausal bone loss.)

Bone loss is most severe in the first 5 to 6 years after menopause and finally slows down at around age 65. Perhaps not coincidentally, about this same time the adrenal glands slow down their production of hormones that stimulate the breakdown of bone.

What Actually Happens

The bone loss that follows menopause is a direct consequence of the body's loss of estrogens. The hallmark of menopause is the dramatic decline in production of the female sex hormones, estrogens and progesterone, by the ovaries. It would therefore seem that these hormones protect the bones in some way and that when their levels drop, the protection is lost.

Bone, however, does not contain receptors for estrogen, as do some other areas of the body (such as the breasts or the lining of the uterus) where the hormones have a definite and direct effect. Scientists have discovered that the effects estrogens have on bone are indirect and are mediated through the body's hormonal control of bone formation and breakdown.

How Estrogen Affects the "Bone Hormones"

Parathyroid Hormone. A normal function of estrogen is to block the bone-dissolving actions of parathyroid hormone. When estrogen levels fall after menopause, the bones become vulnerable to parathyroid hormone. Thus, low levels of parathyroid hormone that would not normally cause bone breakdown actually stimulate bone loss after menopause.

To make matters worse, the calcium released from the broken-down bone turns off the calcium "thermostat" in the parathyroid gland, with the result that more calcium leaves the body than is taken in. The extra calcium comes from the bones. Since bone tissue must be broken down in order to release the calcium, the process leads to a decline of bone mass.

Vitamin D. High levels of estrogens in the body, such as those present during pregnancy, stimulate the activation of vitamin D. But it is not known if a drop in estrogens, as occurs at menopause, will prevent the activation of vitamin D. We do know, however, that osteoporotic postmenopausal women are less able than non-osteoporotic postmenopausal women to complete the last step of vitamin D activation in the kidney.

Calcitonin. Estrogen normally stimulates the secretion of calcitonin (the bone-protecting hormone). This happens both during pregnancy and with estrogen therapy after menopause. Studies so far have been few and inconclusive as to whether or not the loss of estrogen at menopause actually leads to a decline in calcitonin.

How Estrogen Affects Other Hormones

Adrenal Hormones. Overactivity of the adrenal gland is frequently associated with severe osteoporosis. The same is true for long-term use of drugs that resemble adrenal hormones (such as cortisone), even when menopause has not been a factor.

> Adrenal hormones act directly on bone. They attach to receptors on the surfaces of bone cells and cause the bone to respond to the dissolving effects of parathyroid hormone and activated vitamin D.

> Estrogens (prior to menopause) stimulate the liver to produce a protein that binds to certain of the adrenal hormones, lessening their ability to dissolve bone. This effect stops with the loss of estrogens during the early menopausal years, which may account in part for the accelerated loss of bone that occurs at this time.

> Progesterone, the female hormone produced during the second half of the menstrual cycle, is thought to prevent the adrenal hormones from attaching to the bone cell receptors, thus offering further protection to bone. The ovaries stop producing progesterone in the years preceding the menopause, even before they stop producing estrogens.

The adrenal glands slow down their production of bone-dissolving hormones sometime after your 65th year. Some scientists refer to this as the *"adrenopause"* and feel it is the reason that the rate of bone loss decreases at this time.

Growth Hormone. As its name implies, this hormone stimulates growth in many tissues, one of which is bone. Dwarfs have a deficiency of this hormone; giants have an excess of it. We do not know exactly what role growth hormone plays in maintaining the adult skeleton or what effect menopause has on its production. But preliminary research indicates that osteoporotic postmenopausal women are less able to produce growth hormone than are normal postmenopausal women.

Produced by the pituitary gland, growth hormone appears to increase cortical bone formation by stimulating the bone-forming and bone-resorbing cells, which in turn stimulate the bone remodeling cycle.

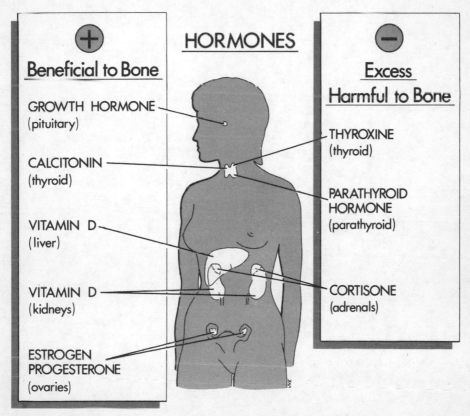

HORMONES INVOLVED IN CALCIUM AND BONE METABOLISM.

Thyroid Hormones. Thyroid hormones play an important
role in the early development of the skeleton. A deficiency of
these hormones in children leads to stunted growth, and an
excess in either children or adults leads to an increase in the
rate of bone remodeling and bone loss.

Other hormonal changes at menopause affect the thyroid
hormones, though these have not been well studied. We know
that estrogens normally stimulate the liver to produce proteins
that bind the thyroid hormones (in a manner similar to the
adrenal hormones). Future research will determine whether or
not the increased amount of "free" thyroid hormone after
menopause is important in terms of bone loss.

4

Will You Get Osteoporosis?

It would be fortunate if we were able to predict just which women are likely to develop osteoporosis. Thus, the 25 percent of the female population who would suffer from the condition could take steps to prevent it while everyone else could safely ignore the problem. Unfortunately, this is not possible. Because osteoporosis is a complex disorder that is rarely caused by a single factor, it is difficult to foretell who will ultimately develop it.

Whether or not you will be affected depends on (1) how much bone you have at maturity, (2) how fast you subsequently lose that bone, and (3) how long you live. Anyone who lives long enough will develop osteoporosis, since a certain amount of bone loss is a normal and inevitable consequence of aging. The other two — how much bone you have at maturity and how fast you subsequently lose that bone — are each influenced by many factors, which may be, to varying degrees, within your control. To assess your risk, and plan for the future, you should know about all of them.

Risk Factors You Cannot Control

Age at Menopause

In general, the earlier your menopause, the greater your risk of osteoporosis. For most women, the end of menstruation and reproductive capacity occurs at around age 50. Of women experiencing a natural menopause, 25 percent will develop osteoporosis.

Removal of your ovaries prior to a natural menopause results in an abrupt and complete loss of estrogens and a 50 percent risk of osteoporosis. The younger you are when you have surgery, the more years you spend without estrogens to protect your bones. Therapy to replace hormones lost after surgery substantially reduces your risk of developing osteoporosis.

Genetic Factors

Get out the family album. Your heredity plays an important role in determining the amount of bone you have at maturity and your rate of bone loss with age. The best evidence for this comes from studies of twins. Identical twins have more closely matched bone mass than fraternal twins, and both types of twins are more closely matched than other siblings. We also know that many, if not most, women with osteoporosis have a family history of the disorder.

Therefore you will want to know your family history. If your grandmother, mother, aunt, or sister has osteoporosis, you are well-advised to consider yourself at high risk. Nevertheless, lack of a family history of the disorder should not give you false confidence, since many other factors can influence your bone mass and your overall risk of osteoporosis.

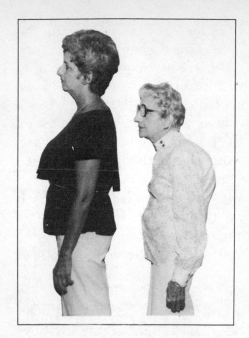

MOTHER AND DAUGHTER. The mother, age 76, has severe osteoporosis. Now only 4′10″, she has lost 5½″ from her early adult height. Her daughter, age 56, has noticed no change from her normal height of 5′4″ and has no outward signs of osteoporosis. Single photon absorptiometry, however, shows that she has a bone mineral content below the average for women of her age, indicating that she may also be developing a tendency toward spontaneous fractures.

Ethnic Differences

Fewer black women develop osteoporosis than white women. Though scientists are not sure of the reasons, there are several factors that may account for this, at least in part.

Black women have larger bones at skeletal maturity. Studies of young children have shown that even early in life there are differences in bone mass between blacks and whites. Black women tend to have larger muscles, and muscle mass and bone mass are closely related (the bigger the muscles, the greater the stress on the bones and the larger the bones).

In addition, black women seem to lose bone with aging at a slower rate. This is probably due to hormonal differences between blacks and whites. There is evidence to suggest, for example, that blacks have higher levels of calcitonin. A recent study at Auburn University of men and women ages 56 to 91 showed that white women tend to lose more calcium in their urine than black women. (The men did not have this racial difference.)

What all this means is that if you are a black woman, you can withstand a greater amount of bone loss before reaching the osteoporotic, fracture-prone state. This is not a total immunity, however. In a recent survey at the University of Florida, 11 percent of women hospitalized for hip fractures were black, although they tended to be much older than the white women with such fractures. A black woman whose ovaries are removed at an early age is theoretically at nearly the same risk as her white, surgically menopausal counterpart, though she has some degree of protection since she started with more bone.

Studies of other ethnic groups have been less extensive. It has been found that women with ancestors from the British Isles, northern Europe, China, or Japan are more likely to develop osteoporosis than are those of African, Hispanic, or

SHOULD YOUR OVARIES BE REMOVED IF YOU ARE HAVING A HYSTERECTOMY?

Hysterectomy — surgical removal of the uterus — is one of the most frequently performed operations on women. Over 650,000 women underwent the procedure in 1981.

Despite these numbers, many women are still confused about just what a hysterectomy is. Strictly speaking, "hysterectomy" means removal of the uterus alone. A "total" or "complete hysterectomy" means removal of the uterus and cervix. When the ovaries are also removed, the procedure is called a "hysterectomy with oophorectomy."

A recent study reported in the *Journal of the American Medical Association* showed that 30 percent of women who had a hysterectomy between the ages of 35 and 44 also had an oophorectomy. Among older women, the percentage was about half. In some of these cases, the ovaries were either diseased or damaged by pelvic inflammation or endometriosis, making removal necessary. However, in a significant number of cases, perfectly normal, healthy ovaries were taken out.

Some physicians routinely recommend that ovaries be removed at the time of hysterectomy, particularly if the patient is around the age of menopause. Their reasoning: since the

Mediterranean ancestry. The risk for Jewish women seems to lie somewhere between the low risk for blacks and the high risk for whites. Overall it appears that *skin pigmentation* is related to risk, and that for white women, the fairer your complexion, the greater your risk.

Bone Structure

Do you wear petite sizes? Small body size, independent of body weight, is a critical risk factor. If you are of petite stature and have the same rate of bone loss as a larger woman, you will reach the osteoporotic, fracture-prone state first, simply because you have less bone to begin with.

woman can no longer have children and the ovaries will soon lose their function at menopause anyway, the surgery will prevent the possibility of ovarian cancer developing at a later date. Though cancer of the ovaries is not common, when it does occur it is often fatal because early diagnosis is difficult (there are no specific tests that can detect it).

While this argument may at first appear sound, it must be placed in perspective. The chances of developing ovarian cancer after a hysterectomy vary from 1 in 100 to 1 in 10,000. By comparison, breast cancer affects 1 in 12 women and colon cancer affects 1 in 25. How many physicians recommend removal of these tissues as a means of preventing future cancer?

We know that 25 to 50 percent of women who have had both ovaries removed prior to a natural menopause will develop osteoporosis at a relatively early age if they do not receive hormone replacement therapy. Does the "benefit" of preventing ovarian cancer outweigh the very real risk of future osteoporosis?

This is the question you must ask your physician *before* your surgery. Discuss the pros and cons of leaving your ovaries alone if they are healthy. If they must be removed, discuss how you will go about preventing the rapid bone loss that follows a surgical menopause.

PATHWAYS TO OSTEOPOROSIS. The upper curve shows women with a normal amount of bone at skeletal maturity (around age 35). All these women will lose bone with age, but 1 out of 4 will become rapid bone losers at the time of menopause and will eventually enter the fracture zone. Even a woman with normal amounts of bone at skeletal maturity can prematurely enter the fracture zone if her ovaries are removed and she does not receive hormone replacement therapy. The lower curve represents women with a subnormal amount of bone at skeletal maturity. Rapid losers in this group will enter the fracture zone sooner than the rapid losers in the normal bone mass group because they started off with less bone. A surgical menopause is particularly detrimental to them.

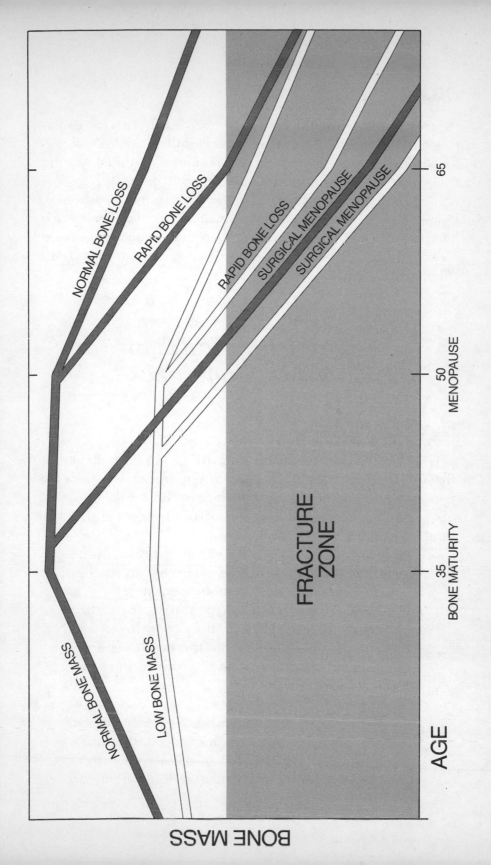

Disease

Several diseases are associated with a high risk of osteoporosis. Most of them are chronic problems in which bone loss is just one of many pathological complications. Among them are certain endocrine disorders (including hyperparathyroidism, hyperthyroidism, and Cushing's syndrome), kidney disease, diabetes, and rheumatoid arthritis. If you have had part of your stomach removed because of cancer or severe ulcers, you are at greater risk because you are less able to absorb calcium from your food.

Risk Factors You Can Control – Sometimes

How's Your Weight?

If you are on the heavy side, you will be comforted to know that obese women rarely develop osteoporosis. Although the reasons for this are not thoroughly understood, we do know that obese women and slender women differ in their abilities to produce estrogens after menopause.

Before menopause, the ovaries produce large amounts of estrogen and progesterone, and smaller amounts of the male sex hormones, androgens. The adrenal glands also produce androgens. After menopause, very small quantities of estrogen and progesterone are produced, but the ovaries and the adrenal glands both continue to produce the same amount of androgens as before.

In fat tissue, these androgens can be chemically converted to estrogen. The more fat a woman has, the more estrogen she can produce. Fat, therefore, substantially reduces her risk of developing osteoporosis. However, before you start doubling up on desserts, you should know that for precisely the same reason, an obese woman has a three to ninefold increased risk of developing cancer of the lining of the uterus (an estrogen-dependent cancer). This is because she is producing estrogen in fat but her ovaries are no longer producing progesterone, which normally protects the lining of the uterus from estrogen overstimulation.

Another factor in the relative immunity obese women enjoy from osteoporosis is that their greater weight places more stress on their bones. Being the adaptable tissue it is, bone responds to increased weight loads by stimulating formation of new bone tissue to meet the greater stress.

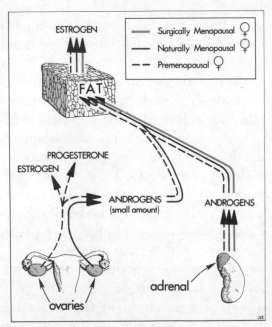

CONVERSION OF ANDROGENS TO ESTROGEN IN FAT. In premenopausal women, most estrogen comes directly from the ovaries, although small amounts are contributed by the conversion of ovarian and adrenal androgens to estrogen in fat. Surgical removal of the ovaries leaves a woman with only adrenal androgens as a source of estrogen. After a natural menopause, the ovaries stop producing estrogen but both the ovaries and adrenal glands continue to produce androgens, which can be converted to estrogen in fat.

Have You Ever Used Oral Contraceptives?

Rarely do you hear about medical benefits of the Pill. There is, however, evidence that women who have used oral contraceptives for long periods of time have stronger bones than women who have not.

Oral contraceptives contain estrogen and progesterone, both of which have positive effects on bone mass. It has been suggested that these hormones in oral contraceptives stimulate the release of calcitonin, which inhibits bone breakdown.

How Many Children Have You Had?

"For every child, a tooth." This old saying, which can apply to bones as well as teeth, does not need to be true. If your daily calcium consumption has been adequate to meet your needs as well as those of your unborn baby, pregnancy can have beneficial effects on bone mass.

The high levels of estrogen during pregnancy stimulate the activation of vitamin D (which promotes calcium absorption) and increase the production of calcitonin (which inhibits bone breakdown). Progesterone also increases dramatically during pregnancy, and this, too, has a bone-conserving effect.

Several studies have verified the beneficial effects of pregnancy on bone. In one group of American women with osteoporosis, two-thirds had never had children. Not enough research has been done to say whether five pregnancies, for example, are more protective than one pregnancy. All we can say conclusively is that your risk of developing osteoporosis is *higher* if you have had *no* children.

In underdeveloped nations, on the other hand, where nutrition is typically poor, pregnancy can have deleterious effects on the mother's skeleton, though this seems to be more true for white than for black women. What little calcium the woman takes in goes straight to the developing baby to build bones. And since the small amount of dietary calcium is usually not even enough to meet the needs of the fetus, the calcium reserves of the mother's skeleton are used as well.

How Well Do You Eat?

Nutrition plays an important role in all aspects of bone physiology. Poor eating habits will prevent normal development of bone in childhood and early adulthood and can accelerate the rate of bone loss as you get older.

But what, exactly, are "good" eating habits? Although overall good nutrition is important, research has shown that the absolute amount of calcium and the relative ratio of calcium to certain other foodstuffs in the diet are the most crucial nutritional determinants of bone health.

Calcium. Although an endocrinologist is apt to describe osteoporosis in women as an estrogen-deficiency problem, which it is, a nutritionist is more inclined to see it as a problem of calcium deficiency (which is also true). Since calcium is such an important component of bone, it is certainly reasonable to assume that a low-calcium diet would compromise bone health.

Laboratory animals fed a diet deficient in calcium develop osteoporosis. Studies of women also show a relationship between low calcium consumption and osteoporosis. In a comparison of bone mass in two groups from different rural areas in Yugoslavia — one group having an average daily calcium intake (940 milligrams) that was twice that of the other (441 milligrams) — it was clear that women in the higher-calcium group definitely had stronger bones at skeletal maturity and a lower incidence of hip fractures later in life than women in the low-calcium group. Studies of American women with osteoporosis have shown these women typically consume less calcium than non-osteoporotic women and, in addition, they absorb it less efficiently from the foods they eat. Studies of British women have corroborated these findings.

With advancing age, everyone experiences a decline in his or her ability to absorb calcium, which is probably one of the reasons we all lose bone as we grow older. Men and women also develop a relative deficiency in *lactase*, the enzyme necessary to digest the sugar lactose found in milk, leading to a decreased consumption of calcium-rich milk and other dairy products. In women, menopause brings on an additional decline in the efficiency of calcium absorption, and this may be another reason women lose more bone than men do.

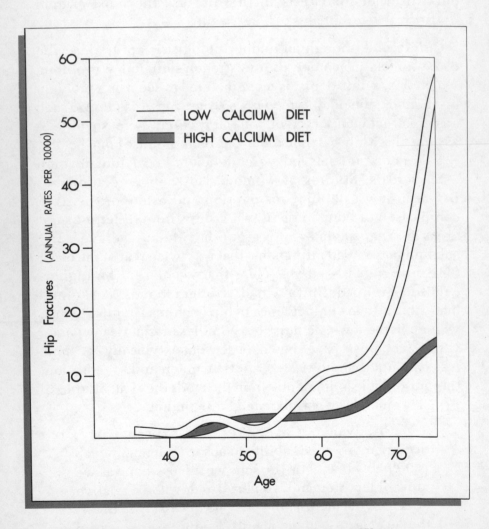

HIP FRACTURE RATES IN YUGOSLAVIAN WOMEN WITH HIGH AND LOW CALCIUM DIETS.

Whatever amount of calcium you take in, if you are menopausal you will absorb less of it and excrete more of it than someone who is premenopausal or someone who is menopausal and receiving estrogen therapy. Thus women need more calcium after menopause than before menopause.

In order to protect your bones at menopause, your calcium requirement jumps from a recommended daily allowance (RDA) of 800 milligrams to at least 1,400 milligrams. Unfortunately, if you are typical, this is a time in your life when you are eliminating the best calcium sources — dairy products — from your diet because they are "too fattening." The average American woman over 45 consumes very little calcium — only 450 milligrams each day. This creates a *negative calcium balance* of about 40 milligrams per day (40 more milligrams of calcium are lost through the urine than are absorbed through the intestines). Translating that into bone loss, she is depleting her bone mass by approximately 1.5 percent per year. At this rate, a woman who experiences menopause at 50 will have lost 15 percent of her bone mass by the time she is 60.

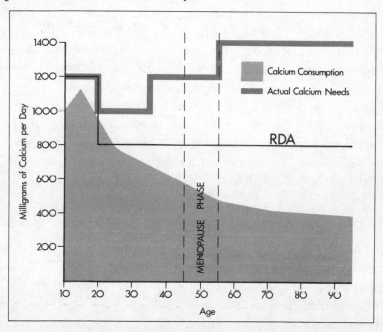

CALCIUM NEEDS AND INTAKE WITH AGE.

Calcium-to-Phosphorus Ratio. Phosphorus is an essential mineral found in every cell of your body and involved in virtually every metabolic process. Along with calcium, phosphorus is a major component of bone. According to some scientists, however, too much phosphorus or, more accurately, phosphorus in excess of calcium, can lead to bone loss.

Studies on animals have demonstrated that when the amount of phosphorus in the diet greatly exceeds the amount of calcium, bone loss can result. This appears to be the case in humans as well, as evidenced by the high rate of bone loss in the Arctic Eskimos of Canada and Alaska, whose diet consists almost exclusively of the phosphorus-rich walrus and seal meats. Arctic Eskimos start losing bone at an earlier age and lose 15 to 20 percent more bone than white Americans.

Estimates of the ratio of phosphorus to calcium in the average American diet range from twice as much to four times as much. Many popular foods, such as bread, cereal, potatoes, red meat, and cola drinks contain much more phosphorus than calcium. Phosphorus is widely used in food additives and is therefore a major component of processed foods. Industry statistics indicate that the typical American gets some 300 milligrams of phosphorus daily from this source alone. For the average woman consuming only 450 milligrams of calcium each day, this leaves a very small theoretical margin of safety.

The exact significance of the effect of phosphorus on calcium and bone loss in humans remains unclear. Some studies have shown that only very large amounts of phosphorus will have an appreciable negative effect. More research needs to be done to determine the ideal calcium-to-phosphorus ratio.

Are You a Vegetarian?

If you have ever considered becoming a vegetarian, but weren't sure it was worth the trouble, you may have your answer now. Vegetarians have stronger, denser bones than people whose diets are heavy with meat. They lose less bone with age, and they develop osteoporosis far less often.

A study comparing older white women who ate meat

regularly to lacto-ovo-vegetarians (cheese and dairy products but no meat) found large differences in the amount of bone lost with age. *Both the meat eaters and the vegetarians had similar amounts of calcium in their diets, yet the meat eaters lost 35 percent of their bone mass between the ages of 50 and 89, whereas the vegetarians lost only 18 percent.* Another study that included both women and men showed increasing differences in bone mass between vegetarians and meat eaters with advancing age. The average bone density of vegetarians in their 70s was greater than that of the meat eaters in their 50s!

Because red meat is rich in phosphorus, the difference in bone mass between vegetarians and meat eaters may be partially explained by the differences in the calcium-to-phosphorus ratios of their diets.

Another part of the explanation has to do with the great difference in acidity: a vegetarian diet has a low acid content, while a meat-containing diet has a high acid content, because meats contain amino acids that are predominantly acidic. Even though it may be some time before scientists have all the answers they are looking for, they do have a theory: they believe that the body responds to an acid overload by dissolving bone tissue in an attempt to neutralize the acidic environment.

Do You Get Enough Exercise?

A funny thing happened on the way to the moon. Healthy young astronauts lost large amounts of calcium from their bones during only a short space flight. The reason? Restricted movement in a gravity-free environment. Similar changes occur in persons confined to wheelchairs or bed rest for as little as several weeks. This condition is called *disuse osteoporosis.* Clearly, you either use your bones or you lose them.

Regular exercise is absolutely critical for development and maintenance of strong, healthy bones. This is true for everyone, from the developing child to the older woman. Exercise is believed to be the only preventive or therapeutic measure that not only halts bone loss but actually stimulates the formation of new bone. Some scientists believe that age-related bone loss is not inevitable but instead related to a decline in physical activity. To the extent that decreased activity with aging is inevitable, then bone loss is also inevitable.

Although the need for exercise is a fact, and most people accept that, scientists are only beginning to study the specific effects of exercise. What type and how much exercise will prevent a woman from losing bone? Or, to take it a step further, if and how much exercise will actually *add* to your bone mass? There are, as yet, no recommended daily allowances for exercise as there are for calcium or vitamin D.

Exercise has beneficial effects on the bones both locally and generally. That is, exercising the legs benefits the bones in the legs and it also benefits the rest of the skeleton, though to a lesser degree. What, exactly, exercise does is not completely understood. However, we do know the following:

1. *Exercise places actual physical stress on bones.* Like muscles, bones respond to stress by becoming bigger and stronger (hypertrophy). And like muscles, they weaken and shrink if they are not used (atrophy).

2. *Exercise increases blood flow to bones, bringing in bone-building nutrients.*

3. *Exercise creates small electrical potentials in bone tissue that stimulate the growth of new bone.*

4. *Exercise affects various components of the body's hormonal control of bone remodeling, somehow shifting the balance toward new bone formation.* In a recently completed study at Pennsylvania State University, middle-aged women, many of whom had never exercised regularly before, were found to have *increased estrogen levels* after a 6-week exercise program. And in another study, middle-aged men who rode exercise bicycles were found to have *lower levels of the harmful adrenal hormones* after they exercised.

So far, most of the studies on the skeletal effects of exercise have concentrated on world-class athletes, comparing them with sedentary individuals. To no one's surprise, the athletes had bigger muscles and denser bones than the inactive persons.

Although few of us are world-class athletes and even fewer of us are willing (or able) to undertake such strenuous training programs to build up our bones, preliminary studies have shown that normal amounts of exercise can have beneficial effects on bones.

In a recent study, the effects of moderate exercise on postmenopausal women (average age was 53) were examined. For 1 year, the women participated in a program recommended by the President's Council on Physical Fitness. Three times a week they did warm-up, circulatory, and conditioning exercises for 1 hour. They did not change their diet. For their efforts, these women were rewarded with a significantly improved calcium balance and *no signs of bone loss.* (However, before it can be concluded that this type of exercise program will prevent osteoporosis, it is necessary to study more women for longer periods of time.)

Investigators conducting a 4-year study now under way in Madison, Wisconsin, hope to determine whether exercise can increase bone mass. One hundred and twenty women approaching their menopausal years are engaged in a program of jazz dancing, isometric exercises, jogging, and square dancing. Preliminary results are encouraging: the exercisers are maintaining their bone mass, while a control group of non-exercising women of the same age have already begun to show the 1 to 2 percent or more yearly loss of bone typical of their age bracket. But whether or not exercising will actually increase bone mass for these women awaits the final results of the study, scheduled for completion in 1984.

Are You a Smoker or Nonsmoker?

In 1972, the smoking habits of a small group of women with severe osteoporosis were examined. It was found that 94 percent were smokers, and of these, 88 percent smoked more than a pack of cigarettes a day. Later, in 1976, the same investigator reported on a larger group (72 women) who had vertebral fractures caused by osteoporosis; 76 percent of this

CAN CONTROLLED WEIGHT-TRAINING PREVENT BONE LOSS AND PROMOTE NEW BONE FORMATION?

As long ago as 1892, it was suggested that mechanical forces acting on bone could cause changes in its architecture. Today researchers at the University of Florida are investigating the effects of a supervised Nautilus exercise program on the bone mass of menopausal women.

The principle of the Nautilus machines is to offer uniform resistance to the force that muscles exert throughout the entire range of their motion. Therefore these exercises can develop the full potential of the muscles. Closely supervised training programs, 20 minutes at a time, three times a week, ensure that workouts are of high intensity, maximum benefit, and minimal risk. Because the exercises are done slowly and deliberately with no jarring or jerking motions, injuries are rare, and wear and tear on the joints, a common problem in jogging, is minimized.

Preliminary results of the University of Florida study, as to whether the Nautilus program can help menopausal women preserve and possibly build up their bone mass, will be reported in 1984.

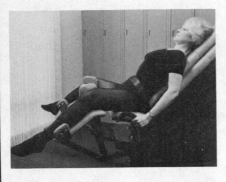 

Exerting force to bring the legs together from the outstretched position exercises the adductor muscle group of the inner thighs.

Extending each leg alternately against a force exercises the major muscle groups of the lower body.

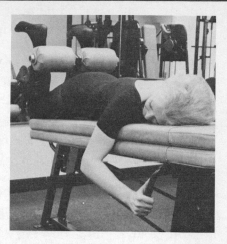

The hamstring muscles of the backs of the thighs bring the legs from the extended position up toward the back of the body.

The pectoralis muscles of the chest bring the arms together in front of the body from the outstretched position.

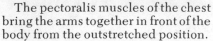

Pulling the overhead horizontal bar down behind the shoulders exercises the major muscles groups of the upper body and arms.

The quadraceps, the large muscles of the tops of the thighs, bring the legs up to the extended position in front of the body.

group were smokers, 68 percent of them heavy smokers.

What does this mean? One possible explanation is related to the effect smoking has on liver function. Since the liver is where vitamin D is activated, it may be that smoking impairs this activation, leading to a decrease in calcium absorption, a more negative calcium balance, and, therefore, a loss of calcium from the bones.

On the other hand, although these studies sound like an indictment of smoking, they really only suggest an *association* between smoking and bone loss. There is no evidence as to whether smoking actually *caused* the women to lose bone more rapidly or whether they simply had lower bone mass at skeletal maturity than the nonsmoking women.

The facts we have shed little light on the subject. We know that women who smoke tend to have an earlier menopause (about 5 years earlier) than nonsmokers. Thus, the smoking connection may be only that a woman who smokes is exposed to more time without estrogen protection for her bones. Or it may be that because smokers are less likely to be overweight (and since obese women are relatively protected from osteoporosis), body weight, and not smoking, is the critical factor here.

The long-term effects of smoking on bone loss in women have been difficult to obtain because women have not been smoking for as long as men. However, more and more women are smoking these days, and they are beginning to do so at an earlier age. Soon there will be a large group of women who have been life-long smokers, and perhaps they will be able to give us the answers on just how smoking and bone loss are linked.

But why wait around for the bad news? We already know that smoking is an important factor in chronic bronchitis, emphysema, lung cancer, and heart disease and contributes to many other diseases. Now is the time to stop smoking!

Do You Drink to Excess?

Alcohol impairs calcium absorption through the intestines, and it may affect the ability of the liver to activate vitamin D.

Excessive use of alcohol blurs the normal distinctions osteoporosis makes between young and old, and men and women. Severe osteoporosis has been seen in male alcoholics who are only in their 20s. Undoubtedly the inadequate nutrition, limited physical activity, and liver damage of many alcoholics contribute to their rapid bone loss.

At this point, not enough research has been done to determine whether moderate amounts of alcohol have any long-term effects on bone mass.

What Medications Do You Take?

There are a number of drugs that are associated with severe bone loss. Many are able to cause osteoporosis by themselves; others merely aggravate an existing tendency to bone loss. In Chapter 6 we discuss what you can do to compensate for the destructive actions of these drugs and what substitutions may be possible.

Corticosteroids. Often used to ameliorate symptoms of rheumatoid arthritis and asthma, the most common corticosteroids are cortisone, hydrocortisone, prednisolone, and dexamethasone. When used for long periods of time these drugs can cause severe loss of bone leading to osteoporosis, irrespective of age or sex.

They appear able to do so in two ways:

1. They create a more negative calcium balance by decreasing calcium absorption and increasing calcium excretion.

2. They act directly on bone tissue to suppress the formation of new bone.

Corticosteroid-induced osteoporosis is in many respects similar to postmenopausal osteoporosis, yet there are distinct differences. In corticosteroid-induced osteoporosis, the degree of bone loss is usually much more severe and the pattern of loss is different, characterized by loss of bone from the ribs and subsequent rib fractures.

Anticonvulsants. Anticonvulsant drugs such as phenytoin, phenobarbital, primidone, and phensuximide are metabolized in the liver. There, they stimulate production of enzymes that break down vitamin D. This leads to a state of relative vitamin D deficiency and, indirectly, a calcium deficiency, since vitamin D is required for calcium absorption. The negative calcium balance caused by anticonvulsants leads to a severe degree of bone loss as the result of both osteomalacia (because of the vitamin D deficiency) and osteoporosis (because of the calcium deficiency).

Antacids. Women constitute an increasing number of the estimated 2.5 million Americans with newly diagnosed ulcers. These women, plus a great number of people who do not have ulcer problems, are daily users of antacids.

With over $110 million spent on antacids each year, they appear to have become part of the American way of life. Most people consider these nonprescription products to be harmless and do not realize that many antacids contain aluminum, which can cause an increase in calcium excretion. This extra calcium comes from the bones.

By themselves, aluminum-containing antacids probably do not cause osteoporosis, but they can contribute to bone loss. Antacids are also often used together with corticosteroids to alleviate gastrointestinal symptoms often associated with their use. And many alcoholics take antacids on a regular basis to soothe their stomachs; this combination has proved destructive in terms of overall bone mass.

Diuretics. Diuretics promote the production of urine and are often prescribed for people with high blood pressure. In terms of their effects on calcium balance and bone mass, some diuretics are good and some are bad.

Furosemide, for example, increases urinary calcium excretion. Thiazides, on the other hand, actually reduce the amount of calcium lost in the urine and are therefore more appropriate for older women.

Thyroid supplements. It is believed that high doses of thyroid supplements produce a physiological state similar to that of overactivity of the thyroid gland, which is known to increase the risk of osteoporosis. A recent study reported that women taking supplements equivalent to or greater than 3 grains of dessicated thyroid (or 300 micrograms of lethothyroxine) had significantly lower bone mass than women who did not take thyroid hormones.

Is Your Water Fluoridated?

A study compared two North Dakota communities, one with a fluoridated water supply and one without. The results showed that the women who drank the water supplemented with fluoride had more bone in their spines than the other group. The effects of fluoride on bone is similar to its effects on teeth — it promotes calcium retention and bone formation.

Check for Pollution

Excessive levels of toxic metals such as cadmium, lead, copper, and zinc in the environment have been associated with bone loss in both farm animals and humans. However, unless you live next door to a zinc-smelting plant, this is probably not going to be a substantial contributor to your risk of osteoporosis.

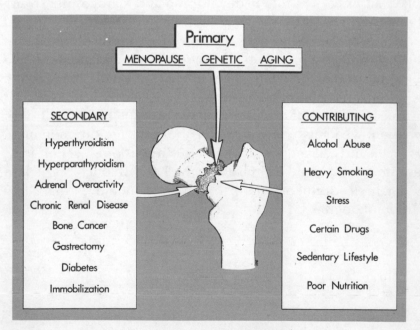

CAUSES OF OSTEOPOROSIS.

Why Don't Men Get Osteoporosis?

A quick scan of nursing home populations will tell you that some men do in fact get osteoporosis. They are a small minority and in general are much older than their female osteoporotic counterparts. Usually, the osteopenia of aging has simply caught up with them, or they may have some secondary risk factor, such as diabetes or long-term use of corticosteroids.

The main reason more men don't get osteoporosis is that, compared with women, they have more bone mass and slower bone loss with age. In addition, compared to women they have higher levels of calcitonin, they generally consume more calcium, and they get more exercise. Men also weigh more and have larger muscles; throughout life they are placing greater stress on their bones, which has positive effects on their bone mass.

Just as the female sex hormones, estrogen and progesterone, protect the bones of women, testosterone (a male sex hormone) plays an important role in developing and maintaining strong bones in men. Unlike women, men do not have a menopausal equivalent that causes a sudden reduction or depletion of testosterone. Aging eventually brings about a gradual decline in testosterone, though the overall decline is not great enough to cause large amounts of bone loss.

Because most of the osteoporosis studies have dealt with women, we know relatively little about the condition in men. We can only assume that the same nutritional, secondary, environmental, and exercise factors that influence the risk in women also influence the risk in men, although perhaps to a different degree.

5

How to Tell If You Are Losing Bone

This is what every woman needs to know. Obviously, you don't want to wait until you have a fracture to find out you are losing bone. You want to stop the progression of bone loss before the substantial harm is done. The question is, how much bone do you have now, and how rapidly are you losing it?

The Problem of Detection

Early detection of osteoporosis has always been extremely difficult. Usually by the time bone loss is apparent to either a woman or her physician, extensive and irreversible damage has already occurred. In its early stages, osteoporosis is a silent disease, exhibiting no outward signs. The problem of detection is complicated by the current lack of a convenient and accurate means of measuring small changes in bone mass. Though sophisticated technologies have been developed that can detect relatively small changes, for the most part these are used only in research and are either prohibitively expensive or not available to the public.

Signs of Bone Loss or Impending Bone Loss

Are You Becoming Shorter?

The first outward sign that you already have osteoporosis is usually loss of height. This may be followed by postural changes and back pain resulting from fracturing, collapse, and crushing of the spinal vertebrae and from the strain on the surrounding ligaments and muscles. Since the bones of your legs do not become shorter, all the height is lost between your hips and neck.

If you do not know exactly how tall you were at skeletal maturity, you can estimate your early adult height by measuring the width of your arm span, since arm span and height are nearly equal in early adulthood. Subtract your arm span from your head-to-heel height to give you a rough indication of your height loss. Accurate measurements of height should be a regular part of all your physical examinations.

Do You Have Transparent Skin?

Look at the back of your hand. Is the skin loose and lacking in pigmentation? Can you see the edges of both the large and small veins? If so, you have transparent skin. (You are also probably over the age of 60, since younger women seldom have transparent skin.) One study of older women with osteoporosis showed that 83 percent had transparent skin on the backs of their hands as opposed to 13 percent with opaque skin.

In 1941 Dr. Fuller Albright, the physician credited with first linking osteoporosis and menopause, noted that many of his osteoporotic patients had transparent skin. Most noticeable on the back of the hand, the transparency is due to a lack of collagen in the skin's outer layers. Since collagen is also a major component of bone, it was reasonable to conclude that "thin skin" is associated with "thin bones."

The thickness of the skin can easily be measured with calipers that pinch the skin on the back of the hand and pull it away from the underlying tissues. There is very little fat in this area, even if you are obese. Using this technique, researchers have found that opaque skin is 35 percent thicker than transparent skin. However, they have not been able to use these facts as a true predictor of osteoporosis. Nevertheless, thin skin should be considered a warning sign of impending or existing osteoporosis.

Do You Have Periodontal Disease?

Periodontal disease (perio = around, dontal = teeth), sometimes called pyorrhea, is a condition involving the supporting tissues of the teeth: the gums, the ligaments attaching the teeth to the jawbone, and sometimes the jawbone itself. It is the major cause of tooth loss in adults and is more common in women than in men, appearing most often in the middle-age years.

In some women, periodontal disease can signal impending osteoporosis. On the other hand, don't jump to the conclusion that a gum problem means you must have bone loss. In many cases, periodontal disease is exactly what it seems — a dental hygiene problem.

How Are Periodontal Disease and Osteoporosis Related?
While a buildup of plaque and subsequent bacterial infiltration

are the major causes of periodontal disease, other factors can be involved.

Loss of bone in the jaw often accompanies periodontal disease. As the jawbone becomes more porous and therefore weaker, the teeth are less firmly anchored. They start moving around, the gums become inflamed and recede, and bacteria are free to invade the open pockets between gums and teeth.

When animals deprived of calcium develop generalized bone loss, it is first evident in their jaw bone, later in their spine, and then in their legs. If the animals are given calcium supplements, bone density in the jaw increases (much more so

ARTHRITIS AND OSTEOPOROSIS: ARE THEY RELATED?

Women with severe rheumatoid arthritis are more likely to have osteoporosis than non-arthritic women of the same age. The nature of this relationship is not clear.

Undoubtedly, long-term use of corticosteroids for treatment of the arthritis is part of the problem, as these drugs are known to cause osteoporosis. But that doesn't explain enough, since even those who have never used corticosteroids have lower bone mass than women who do not suffer from rheumatoid arthritis.

It has also been found that women with rheumatoid arthritis are more likely to have transparent skin than non-arthritic women of the same age (even if they haven't used corticosteroids), and they generally have had arthritis for many more years than those with opaque skin.

We still have a great deal to learn about the relationship between arthritis and osteoporosis. All that can be said at this point is that if you have severe rheumatoid arthritis, your risk of osteoporosis is greater than average, and it is even higher if you have had the disease for many years, if you have received corticosteroids, or if you have transparent skin.

than in the spine or legs).

Similar changes occur in adult humans with habitually low calcium intakes or diets containing more phosphorus than calcium. If they are given daily calcium supplements of 1,000 milligrams, bone density increases and gum inflammation is reduced in as little as 6 months. One study found loss of bone in the jaw to be correlated with loss of bone in the fingers.

Finally, in a study of white women between the ages of 60 and 69, a definite correlation was observed between tooth loss and bone loss elsewhere in the body. Women with reduced cortical bone in their fingers were more likely to have full or partial dentures than women with more cortical bone.

Tests: What Kinds Are Available and How Good Are They?

Blood and Urine Tests

Tests for calcium and other products of bone breakdown are not too helpful in providing a definitive diagnosis of osteoporosis because many women with even severe osteoporosis have perfectly normal levels of these substances in their blood and urine. If you have already experienced bone loss, however, an analysis of bone breakdown products can be helpful in distinguishing bone loss due to osteoporosis from that caused by other bone disorders.

Blood Tests. Since meals result in sporadic elevations of calcium and other compounds in your blood, these tests are performed in the morning after a 12-hour overnight fast. Tests for calcium, phosphorus, and alkaline phosphatase (an enzyme involved in calcium metabolism) are the most common; however, the results of these tests in postmenopausal women are normal, even if the subjects have osteoporosis.

Abnormal levels usually indicate a secondary cause of excessive bone loss, such as overactivity of the parathyroid or thyroid gland. Abnormal levels of alkaline phosphatase may indicate that you have osteomalacia, the bone loss condition linked with vitamin D deficiency.

Urine Tests. Food can also affect the levels of calcium and other compounds in your urine; therefore these tests are performed on freshly voided samples of early morning urine after an overnight fast. The most important tests are the *calcium-to-creatinine ratio* (reflects loss of calcium from the bones) and the *hydroxyproline-to-creatinine ratio* (reflects loss of collagen from bone). Some physicians use a 24-hour analysis of calcium in the urine. Here again, abnormal values are indicative of a secondary cause of bone loss.

Spinal or Hip X-Rays

X-rays of the spine or hip are commonly used, but they are not sensitive enough to detect bone loss early enough to do any good. More than 30 percent of bone mass must be lost before even the most experienced radiologist can detect osteoporosis. All that X-rays can do is tell you that you have osteoporosis after it is too late to prevent it. They are, however, valuable for determining the degree of damage caused by existing osteoporosis.

Radiogrammetry

The sensitivity of the X-ray technique can be enhanced by making precise measurements of the width of a bone's cortical shell. With radiogrammetry, the bone of the middle finger between the wrist and knuckles (the metacarpal) is typically used. The identified width of the bone marrow cavity is subtracted from the total width of the bone to yield an estimate of the cortical thickness.

The advantages of radiogrammetry are that it is easy to perform, it requires no special or expensive equipment, it delivers a small dose of radiation to a small area of the body, and it can be easily and safely repeated at specific intervals to estimate the rate of bone loss.

Unfortunately, radiogrammetry is still too insensitive a measure of bone mass to serve as a screening tool for osteoporosis. While it gives a rough estimate of cortical bone loss, it cannot measure changes in trabecular bone and is therefore of no value in predicting spinal bone loss.

Radiographic Photodensitometry

Photodensitometry is a more sophisticated technique for determining the density of bone from X-rays. The bones of the middle segment of the fingers (the phalanges) are used for this test.

A small piece of aluminum alloy is placed next to the hand while the X-ray is taken. Afterward, a computer scans small sections of the X-ray, one at a time, and compares the density of the bone to the known density of the aluminum alloy. While radiographic photodensitometry is ten times more accurate than visual inspection of X-rays, it suffers from the same drawbacks as radiogrammetry: it cannot measure trabecular bone and it cannot predict bone loss in the spine.

Another disadvantage of this method is that special equipment is needed for interpreting the results; therefore most physicians and hospitals cannot use photodensitometry for their patients.

There is, however, a service offered by the Clinical Radiology Testing Laboratory of Miami Valley Hospital in Yellow Springs, Ohio. They will send your physician the aluminum alloy with careful instructions on how to perform the X-ray. The X-ray is then mailed to the Ohio lab, and it in turn will send your physician a report describing your bone density in relation to other women of various ages.

Your physician can obtain more information about the service by writing to Clinical Radiology Testing Laboratory, Miami Valley Hospital, King's Yard, P.O. Box 478, Yellow Springs, Ohio 45387.

X-Rays of the Jaw

Since bone loss in the jaw may precede and therefore warn of bone loss elsewhere in the body, dentists are in a unique position to identify some women at risk of osteoporosis. X-rays of the jaw can therefore be helpful as a screening device. If your dentist tells you that you have reduced bone density in your jaw, you may be at increased risk of osteoporosis.

Single Photon Absorptiometry

This technique has been used in research for many years and is one of the most widely accepted methods of precise and accurate determination of bone mineral content and bone width. A *densitometer* measures the mineral content in the bones of the forearm (the radius and ulna) by calculating how many gamma rays are absorbed — the greater the absorption, the greater the bone mineral content and the greater the bone density.

The procedure is simple. Two lines are drawn on your forearm, marking specific points on the mid and lower portions of the radius; then the scanner is positioned to measure the bone density at these points. The instrument incorporates a computer that calculates the results and prints them out in graph form. The test is painless, takes less than 10 minutes, and exposes you to less than one one-hundredth (1/100) the amount of radiation of an ordinary arm X-ray.

The densitometer is sensitive enough to detect a 1 percent to 3 percent loss of bone (versus 30 percent with X-rays). It is especially accurate at the midpoint of the arm, an area which has a correlation with the total weight of the skeleton, the total amount of calcium in the body, and the amount of bone in the femur (the hip bone).

Like the other techniques, single photon absorptiometry has the drawback of correlating only moderately with the actual amount of bone in the spine. This is because the midpoint of the radius is mostly cortical bone. (Measurement of the lower end of the radius — where 26 percent of the bone is trabecular — reflects the condition of the spine more accurately, though in this position the densitometer results are less reproduceable.)

An additional disadvantage is the cost of the instrument and its relative unavailability. We hope that in the near future medical groups and community health centers will pool their resources to make this valuable screening device available to more women.

Single photon absorptiometry offers a simple and non-invasive measure of skeletal status with high precision and accuracy. Further technical advances may make the instrument more useful for predicting early changes in the spine.

THE CENTER FOR CLIMACTERIC STUDIES OSTEOPOROSIS SCREENING PROGRAM

At the Center for Climacteric Studies at the University of Florida, the single photon absorptiometry method has been used successfully for screening asymptomatic persons and for monitoring patients on treatment to determine their response to treatment. Of 250 "at risk" women (ages 20 through 80) screened to date, 53 percent were found to have lower than average amounts of bone, and 21 percent were actually found to have osteoporosis.

The bone mineral content test is combined with blood and urine tests and a dietary and medical history. Depending upon the results, repeat measurements are taken every 3, 6, or 12 months, making it possible to calculate the rate at which bone is being lost. If the calculated rate exceeds the norm, specific therapy is recommended or the existing treatment program is reassessed and upgraded.

The densitometer is also used to discriminate between cortical (mid-radius) and trabecular (lower radius) bone loss. Persons with reduced lower radius values are then screened for vertebral bone loss with dual photon absorptiometry, which is a much more sensitive measure of trabecular bone.

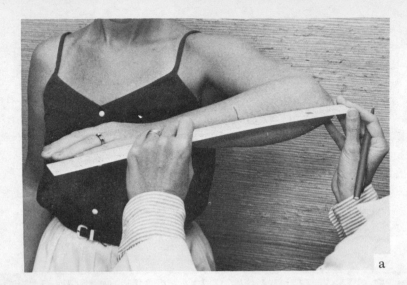

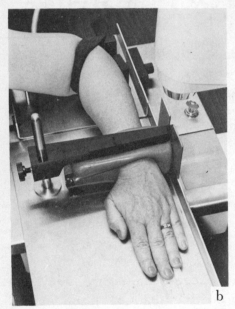

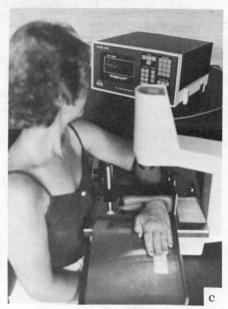

THE SINGLE PHOTON ABSORPTIOMETRY METHOD FOR ASSESSING BONE LOSS. (a) The patient's forearm is measured and marked so that perfect alignment with the densitometer scanner is possible. (b) After aligning the mark with the appropriate position on the densitometer, the patient's arm is firmly strapped in to minimize movement, which would decrease the accuracy of the measurement. (c) The upper part of the densitometer (foreground) moves toward the patient and then back again, scanning the bone and calculating

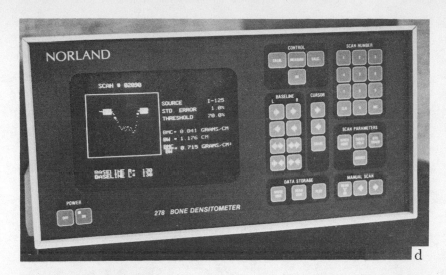

d

e

the bone mineral content, which is then displayed on the screen of the computer module (background). (d) A close-up of the computer module screen showing the results of the bone mineral content determination. (e) The patient's bone mineral content is plotted on a standardized graph (developed by E. Smith and J. R. Cameron of the University of Wisconsin Bone Mineral Laboratory) so that she can compare her bone mass with other women of her own age.

CAT Scan

The most accurate method of determining early loss of bone in the spine is with a specially modified CAT-scanner, which can measure the exact amount of trabecular bone within an individual vertebra. The procedure can be completed in about 30 minutes; the measurement is usually taken at the mid-portion of the first and second lumbar (low back) vertebrae.

There are some disadvantages. The CAT scan exposes you, including your internal organs, to relatively high amounts of radiation. In addition, the test is expensive, and CAT scan units are generally unavailable for screening asymptomatic populations.

Dual Photon Absorptiometry

This is a relatively new and potentially practical method of measuring trabecular bone content in the spine. The principle is similar to that of single photon absorptiometry. The densitometer uses an isotope with two different energies to measure accurately the density of bone situated in deeper tissues.

Although accepted in clinical research, the technique is only just now being introduced into medical practice, and relatively few centers can provide the service to women. As with single photon absorptiometry, radiation exposure is minimal. The test takes 35 to 60 minutes and will probably be intermediate in cost between single photon absorptiometry and a CAT scan.

Summary

There are a number of methods available for screening women for osteoporosis. Hand X-rays assess cortical bone only and are the least accurate of all the testing procedures. However, they are the most readily available; virtually every community has a unit capable of taking hand X-rays, and, if necessary, the X-ray can be mailed for specialist interpretation.

Single photon absorptiometry offers a much more sensitive

measurement of cortical bone and is very practical and safe for large-scale screening and monitoring of treatment. Its main limitations are that it is less accurate in measuring trabecular (as opposed to cortical) bone and it is not yet readily available to the public. The technique is being modified to allow more accurate measurements of the bone mineral content of the lower radius (which correlates with that of the spine), which will probably make this the instrument of choice for screening.

Dual photon absorptiometry shows promise as a means of identifying women at risk of losing bone in their spines. For the most part, this technique is still being used only in research and in a very few clinical centers; it will probably be several years before it is available as a clinical service to the public.

CAT scans may be the most accurate means of assessing bone loss in the spine, but the enormous cost of CAT scan units and the relatively large amounts of radiation the patient is exposed to will probably preclude them from being used on a large scale to screen women for osteoporosis.

To find out what is available in your community, call your County Medical Society. It should be able to tell you exactly what equipment is being used in area medical groups, hospitals, and research centers. Keep in mind that, as with the diagnosis of so many other conditions, one single test can rarely give a definitive answer. Also, to assess how rapidly you are losing bone, at least two measurements of your bone mass are needed. How frequently you require assessment will depend on the number of "at-risk" factors you have, on the sensitivity of the technique and, of course, on the cost and availability of the technique.

6

How to Prevent Osteoporosis

"An ounce of prevention is worth a pound of cure." These words almost seem to have been written about osteoporosis. Armed with information on nutrition, exercise, bone mass tests, and hormone therapy, every woman should be able to protect herself from osteoporosis. Nutrition and exercise strategies may require changes from your usual habits, but they will all be sound, health-promoting changes.

Get Enough Calcium

Some people believe that milk is only for babies and children. Wrong! We all need milk, or at least the calcium it provides, throughout our lives. The recommended daily allowance (RDA) of calcium for adults is 800 milligrams. Although the RDA is set well above the average requirement, the amount that you need will depend upon your health, diet, menopausal status, and age.

Most American women consume a mere 450 milligrams of calcium each day and are unaware of just how deficient their diets are. We now know that if you are over 35, you need much more calcium than you did as a young adult. Because of the hormonal changes that precede and follow menopause, you need at least 1,200 to 1,400 milligrams of calcium daily just to stay in calcium balance.

Do you know if you are getting enough calcium? To find out, keep a record of all the foods you eat for 1 week. Or, to make the job easier, only record the calcium-rich foods. (Use the calcium diary at the back of this book.) At the end of the week, use the calcium chart to calculate the total amount of calcium you have taken in, dividing this number by seven to obtain an average daily consumption. If your daily intake falls short of the figures below, you will need to make changes in your diet.

AGE	REQUIREMENT
Before menopause	800 to 1,000 milligrams
During or after menopause	1,200 to 1,400 milligrams

Stay In Calcium Balance

Calcium balance is the net of the processes through which calcium enters and leaves the body. If you take in and absorb more calcium than you lose (through your sweat, urine, or feces), then you are in *positive calcium balance.* If, on the other hand, you lose more than you take in, you are in *negative calcium balance.*

Remaining in negative calcium balance for very long can cause you to lose large amounts of bone — your body leaches calcium from your skeleton to make up for its losses. It has been estimated that 25 years of a negative calcium balance can

CALCIUM CONTENT OF SOME COMMON FOODS

Food	Amount	Ca(mg)
DAIRY PRODUCTS		
Milk		
Whole, 3.5%	1 cup	288
Nonfat (skim)	1 cup	296
Butter, stick	½ cup	23
Buttermilk	1 cup	296
Cheese		
Blue or Roquefort	1 cu in	54
Camembert	1 wedge	40
Cheddar	1 cu in	129
Cottage	12 oz	320
Parmesan, grated	1 tbsp	68
Swiss (natural)	1 cu in	139
Swiss (processed)	1 cu in	159
American	1 cu in	122
Cream		
Half-and-half	1 tbsp	16
Light	1 tbsp	15
Sour	1 tbsp	12
Custard, baked	1 cup	297
Ice cream	1 cup	194
Ice milk		
Hardened	1 cup	204
Soft-serve	1 cup	273
Margarine, stick	½ cup	23
Pudding		
Chocolate	1 cup	250
Vanilla	1 cup	298
Yogurt		
made from whole milk	1 cup	272
made from partially skimmed milk	1 cup	294
MEAT, POULTRY AND SEAFOOD		
Beef, lean only	2½ oz	10
Chicken breast, fried	2½ oz	9
Eggs		
Whole	1 egg	27
Yolk of egg	1 yolk	24
Scrambled with milk and fat	1 egg	51
Clams	3 oz	53
Crabmeat, canned	3 oz	38
Haddock, breaded, fried	3 oz	34
Oysters, raw	1 cup	226

Food	Amount	Ca(mg)
Salmon, pink, canned	3 oz	167
Sardines, canned in oil, drained	3 oz	372
Shrimp, canned	3 oz	98
Soups		
Canned (prepared with water)		
Clam chowder	1 cup	34
Cream of chicken	1 cup	24
Cream of mushroom	1 cup	41
Minestrone	1 cup	37
Tuna, canned in oil, drained	3 oz	7
VEGETABLES		
Asparagus, green	1 cup	37
Beans		
Lima	1 cup	80
Red kidney	1 cup	74
Snap (green or yellow)	1 cup	72
Beets	1 cup	29
Broccoli, cooked	1 stalk	158
Brussels sprouts	1 cup	50
Cabbage		
Raw	1 cup	39
Cooked	1 cup	64
Red, raw, coarsely shredded	1 cup	29
Carrots	1 cup	45
Cashew nuts	1 cup	53
Cauliflower, cooked	1 cup	25
Celery, pieces	1 cup	39
Collards, cooked	1 cup	289
Mustard greens, cooked	1 cup	193
Onions		
Raw	1 onion	30
Cooked	1 cup	50
Parsnips, cooked	1 cup	70
Peanuts, roasted	1 cup	107
Peas, green	1 cup	44
Pumpkin, canned	1 cup	57
Sauerkraut, canned	1 cup	85
Spinach	1 cup	200
Squash, cooked	1 cup	55
Sweet potatoes	1 med	52
Tomatoes	1 med	24

Food	Amount	Ca(mg)	Food	Amount	Ca(mg)
Tomato catsup	1 cup	60	Farina, cooked	1 cup	147
Turnips, cooked	1 cup	54	Muffins, enriched		
Turnip greens,			white flour	1 muffin	42
cooked	1 cup	252	Oats	1 cup	44
			Oatmeal	1 cup	22

FRUITS AND FRUIT PRODUCTS

Food	Amount	Ca(mg)	Food	Amount	Ca(mg)
			Pancakes		
Apricots			Wheat flour	1 cake	27
Canned in heavy			Plain or buttermilk	1 cake	58
syrup	1 cup	28	Pie		
Dried, uncooked	1 cup	100	Butterscotch	4 in sec	98
Avocados	1		Custard	4 in sec	125
	medium	26	Mince	4 in sec	38
Blackberries, raw	1 cup	46	Pecan	4 in sec	55
Blueberries, raw	1 cup	21	Pumpkin	4 in sec	66
Cantaloupes, raw,			Pizza, cheese	5½ in sec	107
medium	½ melon	27	Rice, cooked	1 cup	21
Cherries, canned,			Rolls		
red	1 cup	37	Frankfurter or		
Dates, pitted	1 cup	105	hamburger	1 roll	30
Grapefruit, pink	½ med	20	Hard	1 roll	24
Grapefruit juice	1 cup	23	Spaghetti with meat		
Grape juice (canned			balls		
or bottled)	1 cup	28	Home recipe	1 cup	124
Lime juice	1 cup	22	Canned	1 cup	53
Oranges	1 med	54	Waffles		
Orange juice	1 cup	26	Enriched flour	1 waffle	85
Papayas, raw	1 cup	36	From mix	1 waffle	179
Peaches, dried	1 cup	77			
Pineapple	1 cup	27			

SUGARS AND SWEETS

Food	Amount	Ca(mg)
Pineapple juice,		
canned	1 cup	37
Plums, canned	1 cup	36
Prunes, cooked	1 cup	60
Prune juice, bottled	1 cup	36
Raspberries, raw	1 cup	27
Rhubarb, cooked	1 cup	212
Strawberries, raw	1 cup	31
Tangerines	1 med	34
Watermelon	4 in wedge	30

Food	Amount	Ca(mg)
Caramels	1 oz	42
Chocolate, milk,		
plain	1 oz	65
Fudge, plain	1 oz	22
Molasses,		
blackstrap	1 tbsp	137
Sherbet	1 cup	31
Sugar, brown	1 cup	187

GRAIN PRODUCTS

Food	Amount	Ca(mg)
Barley	1 cup	32
Biscuits, home		
made	1 biscuit	34
Bran flakes with		
raisins	1 cup	28
Bread	1 slice	23
Cakes (from mixes)	1 piece	55
Cupcakes (from		
mixes)	1 small	43
Cornmeal	1 cup	23

NUTS AND BEANS

Food	Amount	Ca(mg)
Almonds	½ cup	160
Pecans	½ cup	42
Tofu (soybean curd)	3½ oz	128
Walnuts	½ cup	50

Adapted from: Krause MV, Mahan LK. Food, nutrition and diet therapy. Philadelphia: WB Saunders Co, 1979: 828.

consume one-third of your skeleton. Positive calcium balance is essential for healthy bones and to prevent excessive bone loss.

A body normally absorbs only about 10 to 30% of the calcium it obtains from food. How much your body absorbs, as well as how much it excretes, are affected by a number of both dietary and nondietary factors. By learning what these factors are and how your body handles calcium, you can help yourself stay in positive calcium balance.

Good Sources of Calcium

Milk is the ideal calcium source. It not only contains a whopping 291 milligrams of calcium per cup, but it is fortified with vitamin D to ensure absorption of the calcium, and it contains lactose, a sugar that also aids in calcium absorption. Hard cheeses (such as Swiss, brick, or cheddar) contain more calcium per serving than soft cheeses (cottage cheese, for example). Other foods high in calcium are tofu, red salmon, sardines, nuts, broccoli, and many leafy green vegetables.

Although dairy products are the principal source of calcium in our culture, this is not the case elsewhere around the globe. The Chinese, for instance, depend on soybean products and leafy green vegetables. If you have any doubts about green vegetables as a source, consider where the dairy cow gets the calcium she gives us!

Calcium in Your Water. If you live in an area with "soft" water, you can get 10 to 30 milligrams of calcium per quart of tap water. If you have "hard" water, you can get up to 100 milligrams per quart.

Discover Tofu

Tofu, a popular food among vegetarians and health food enthusiasts, is an excellent source of calcium. This mild, low-fat, no-cholesterol, nutritious, cheese-like food is made by pressing the curds of soybean milk into blocks.

A single 3½ ounce serving contains 128 milligrams of calcium, 78 grams of protein, and only 72 calories. It is also a good source of iron, potassium, the essential B vitamins, and vitamin E.

Described as a "culinary chameleon," tofu takes on the flavors and seasonings of anything it is cooked with. It can be eaten plain without cooking, or used as an ingredient in soups, stews, salads, vegetable or egg dishes, or desserts. There are many new cookbooks that can show you how easy it is to prepare tofu and to include it as a regular part of your diet.

Look for tofu in the produce section of your grocery store or in health food stores. Always buy the freshest you can find and avoid the canned tofu, as it tends to be bitter and rubbery.

If you have never tried tofu, you are in for a real treat!

"But I Can't Drink Milk"

Perhaps you are one of the thirty million Americans who cannot drink milk without suffering from diarrhea, cramps, and gas. This problem, called *lactase deficiency* or *lactose intolerance*, is due to lack of the intestinal enzyme *lactase*, which splits the sugar *lactose*, found in milk and other dairy products, into easily digested fractions.

Lactase deficiency is a common problem in the United States, affecting 24 percent of whites and 80 percent of blacks. It also affects a high proportion of Eskimos, Asians, American Indians, Orientals, and South Americans. (The high incidence of lactose intolerance in black women coupled with their low incidence of osteoporosis suggests that ethnic protection overrides the risk imparted by the lactase deficiency.)

Among white women, lactase deficiency is nine times more prevalent in those with osteoporosis, suggesting that in the absence of ethnic protection, lactase deficiency may be a significant risk factor for osteoporosis.

Milk, ice cream, pudding, and other milk products contain large amounts of lactose. Cheese contains somewhat less, although the amount varies considerably with the type. Gouda and Edam are lower than most and are generally better tolerated. Yogurt contains less lactose than milk (but slightly more than some cheeses) and may be tolerated in small amounts.

If you suffer from lactase deficiency, you have three options. You can eliminate all lactose-containing foods from your diet and depend entirely on other food sources for your calcium. (Most people find this hard to do, which is probably why the incidence of lactase deficiency among osteoporotics is so high.) Second, you can eliminate all dairy products and use calcium supplements. This is the easiest and most reliable way of getting enough calcium. Your third option is to try one of the commercially available products that supply the missing enzyme. These are usually powders or liquids that can be added to a quart of milk. Several types are available. If you can't find them in your grocery store, try the health food stores.

Tips to Enhance the Calcium in Your Meals

1. Make your own soup. Not only is this easier than you may think, but the gustatory, nutritional, and financial rewards are well worth the effort. If you add a small amount of vinegar when preparing stock from bones, the vinegar will dissolve the calcium out of the bones, making a single pint of your homemade soup equal to a quart or more of milk in calcium content. The vinegar also tenderizes the meat and reduces the cooking time. As the stock is boiled, the calcium combines with the vinegar and the taste of the vinegar disappears. If any vinegar odor remains, remove the lid and allow the odor to boil off before adding the vegetables.

2. The same principle can be applied to cooking bone-containing meats. Use vinegar to tenderize the meat before cooking. The cooking time will be reduced, and the vinegar taste will disappear. The juices that remain after cooking should be used for gravy, as they contain much of the dissolved calcium.

3. Substitute shredded or grated cheese for butter on vegetables. Parmesan cheese is especially good for adding both calcium and good taste.

4. Cubes of cheese or tofu can be added as a garnish to many soups or salads to enhance their taste and nutritional value.

5. When making a salad, use the deep green lettuce leaves, as these are much richer than the paler leaves not only in calcium but in vitamins A, C, E, and B, folic acid, and many other minerals.

6. When pickling fruits or vegetables, use calcium chloride instead of sodium chloride (table salt). Calcium chloride is more effective and more nutritious.

7. Add powdered nonfat dry milk to everything you can. It makes skim milk, coffee, and tea "thicker" and creamier, and enhances the flavor of cream soups and casseroles. Every teaspoon you use gives you 50 milligrams of calcium and *no fat*.

8. When baking bread, cake, cookies, or muffins, add powdered nonfat milk (about ¼ cup) to the recipe to boost the calcium content — you'll get more calcium and you'll never know it's there!

Calcium Without the Calories

Many women have a chronically low calcium intake because they are trying to avoid what they consider "high calorie" dairy products. Taking calcium supplements to meet your daily need of 1,200 to 1,400 milligrams is an excellent alternative.

There are many different types of calcium supplements on the market, all of which are available over-the-counter without a physician's prescription. Be sure to read the label to find out just how much calcium is in each tablet, so you take the proper number each day.

Calcium is best absorbed in small amounts, so if you use calcium supplements, try to space them out during the day. It is best to take them between meals with a small glass of milk or a bit of yogurt; the vitamin D and lactose in these products will help you absorb more of the calcium. Save about one-third of your daily dose for just before bedtime because the body loses larger amounts of calcium when you sleep. This is because you are fasting and immobile — two states which signal the body to extract calcium from the bones.

Listed below are amounts of different types of foods needed to supply the amount of calcium found in one cup of milk. Some of these may be easy to substitute for milk; others are simply ridiculous. While you may find a few practical substitutions on the list, you can see how hard it is to get all the calcium you need from your diet if your intake of dairy products is low.

Dairy Products	Approx Measure	
Buttermilk	1	cup
Cheese, American pasteurized process ..	1½ oz	
Cheese, Cheddar	1½ oz	
Cheese, Cottage creamed and lowfat ..	2	cups
Cheese, Cottage, dry curd	6	cups
Cheese, Swiss	1	oz
Cheese Food, American	2	oz
Cheese Spread, American	2	oz
Half-and-Half	1	cup
Ice Cream, Vanilla	1¾ cups	
Milk, Chocolate	1	cup
Milk, Dry Whole; 1 oz to 8 oz of water.......	1	cup
Milk, Evaporated, as is	½	cup
Milk, Evaporated, 1 part to 1 of water	1	cup
Milk, Instant Nonfat Dry; 3.2 oz to 1 qt of water	1	cup
Milk, Lowfat	1	cup
Milk, Skim	1	cup
Milk, Sweetened Condensed, as is	⅓	cup
Milk, Sweetened Condensed, 1 part to 1.5 water	1	cup
Pudding, Chocolate ...	1	cup
Yogurt	1	cup

Meat, Poultry, Fish, Eggs, and Peanut Butter

Beef, Roast	5	lb
Chicken, Fried	4½	lb
Eggs	10	
Frankfurters	97	
Ham, baked	5	lb
Meat Patties	5½	lb
Peanut Butter	29	tbsp
Perch, Fried, Breaded .	2	lb
Pork Chops	6	lb
Salmon, Red, with Bones and Oil	4	oz
Sardines	2¼ oz	
Tuna	7¾ lb	

Combination Foods

Beans, Baked, Pork and Tomato Sauce	2	cups
Custard, Baked........	1	cup
Macaroni and Cheese..	¾	cup
Pizza, Cheese	¼ of 14″ pie	
Soup, Cream of Tomato	1¾ cups	
Tacos, Beef	1½	

Fruits and Vegetables	Approx Meas	
Apples, medium	29	
Bananas, medium	29	
Beans, Green	4¾ cups	
Beans, Lima	3¾ cups	
Broccoli	2	cups
Cabbage	1½ heads	
Carrots, 5″ long	15	
Corn	36	cups
Greens (collards, kale, mustard, turnip)	1	cup
Oranges, medium	5	
Orange Juice	13	cups
Peas, Green	10	cups
Potatoes, Baked, large .	22	
Potatoes, French-fried .	448	pieces
Potatoes, Sweet medium	7	
Strawberries	9	cups
Tomatoes, medium	11	
Watermelon..........	21	cups

Grains

Bread, White, slices, enriched	15	
Bread, Whole Wheat, slices	13	
Cornbread, 2½″x3¼″, enriched	3	pieces
Cornflakes (without milk)	73	cups
Crackers, Saltines	485	crackers
Noodles, Egg, enriched	18	cups
Oatmeal	13	cups
Rice	14	cups
Rolls, Frankfurters or Hamburger	10	
Rolls, Hard	12	
Tortillas, Corn, 6″ diameter, enriched ...	5	
Waffles, 3½″x5½″, enriched	5	

Others

Bar, Milk Chocolate ...	4½ oz	
Beer.................	6	qts
Butter	3	lb
Cake, Devil's Food	½ of 9″ cake	
Cake, Sponge	1 10″ cake	
Coffee, Black	73	cups
Cookies, Sugar	18	
Doughnuts, Cake-Type	22	
Mayonnaise...........	6	cups
Pie, Apple	4 9″ pies	
Popcorn, Plain	291	cups
Potato Chips	364	
Sherbet, Orange.......	10	cups
Wine, Rose	2	qts

Which Calcium Supplement Is Best?

Calcium supplements are recommended as an easy way to ensure a proper amount of calcium in your diet. There is an overwhelming variety of products available in tablet, powder, and liquid forms. Some are combined with vitamin D (to aid in absorption), some are combined with magnesium and other minerals, and some come in multivitamin form.

To add to the confusion, different formulations contain different amounts of calcium. For instance, 1,000 milligrams of calcium carbonate contain 400 milligrams of calcium, whereas 1,000 milligrams of calcium lactate contain only 130 milligrams of calcium.

As far as we know, it doesn't seem to matter which compound you take, as long as you get the proper amount of calcium. If the label doesn't give you enough information about the formula, ask your physician or pharmacist.

Some things you should know about calcium supplements:

Calcium carbonate is usually the least expensive and supplies the highest amount of calcium per tablet.

Calcium lactate should not be used if you are lactose intolerant.

Calcium chloride is good for pickling but bad as a supplement as it tends to irritate the stomach.

Calcium gluconate may be too sweet for some people and contains such a small amount of calcium (10 milligrams per 1,000 milligrams) it must be taken frequently during the day.

Calcium levulinate also has a low percentage of calcium (130 milligrams per 1,000 milligrams) and has a bitter, salty taste.

Other products include *calcium ascorbonate, calcium orotate,* and *chelated calcium.*

Bone meal and *dolomite* are high in calcium but controversial as calcium supplements because they may be contaminated with toxic metals (lead, cadmium, and others). The significance of this is still unclear. One teaspoon of bone meal contains 120 milligrams of calcium and 1 teaspoon of dolomite contains 1,180 milligrams of calcium.

The Importance of Vitamin D

Vitamin D, the "sunshine vitamin," is critical for the creation of new bone after breakdown (calcium absorption and bone mineralization cannot take place without it). The recommended daily allowance for adults is 400 international units, which may be obtained either from your diet or from the sun.

Although the sun is an excellent source of vitamin D, there is no way to measure how much you are getting. The amount of vitamin D you receive depends on the length of time you are exposed to the sun, on the sun's intensity, and on atmospheric conditions. It has been estimated that a white woman needs about 15 minutes to 1 hour of sunshine daily to meet her vitamin D requirement. Only you can judge whether or not you are getting enough sunshine on a regular basis.

Vitamin D in the diet is fairly limited: fatty fish, butter, eggs, liver, and milk are the best sources. Milk itself has little vitamin D, but most commercial milk is now fortified with 400 units per quart.

Vitamin D deficiency is not uncommon but is totally unnecessary, as most multivitamin preparations contain the 400 units you need each day. By getting enough vitamin D you ensure adequate absorption of calcium and prevent osteomalacia, the bone disease that can contribute to the bone loss of osteoporosis. However, don't become overzealous: too much vitamin D can actually stimulate bone loss. The American Society for Bone and Mineral Research recommends avoiding amounts in excess of 1,000 units per day.

Can I Take Too Much Calcium?

Many people are afraid that "excess" milk consumption (or sometimes any milk at all) will lead to kidney stones. They naturally feel the same about calcium supplements.

While it is true that a *very high* consumption of calcium can increase your risk of kidney stones, quantities under 2,000 milligrams daily constitute a very small risk. On the other hand, if you have a history of kidney stones, it is necessary to consult your physician before taking large amounts of calcium.

Calcium and High Blood Pressure

There is increasing evidence that high blood pressure (hypertension) may be associated with a low calcium diet and low levels of ionized calcium in the blood. Conversely, calcium supplements may protect against an elevation of blood pressure. Most of the research has been done in laboratory animals, but a few studies, including a very recent one, have shown this relationship to also be true for humans.

Around the world, high blood pressure is more common in areas with low calcium than high calcium consumption. And one study in this country reported that, on the average, persons with hypertension take in less dietary calcium than those with normal blood pressure.

Since calcium supplements have been found to lower blood pressure in both laboratory animals and humans, the calcium supplements you use for protecting against bone loss may help to protect you from hypertension as well.

Beware of the "Bone Robbers"!

Protein. This normally beneficial part of your diet can sometimes have a negative effect on calcium balance. In the past, an increase in protein was recommended for women who already had osteoporosis because it was thought to improve calcium absorption. We now know that protein increases calcium excretion more than it increases calcium absorption, *thus leading to an overall loss of calcium from the body.*

Calcium loss caused by protein is quick, dramatic, and clinically significant in terms of bone loss. In a study of women whose average protein intake was 65 grams per day (roughly equivalent to the protein in three hamburgers), a 50 percent increase in protein caused the loss of an extra 26 milligrams of calcium per day; translated into bone loss, this is approximately a 1 percent loss of bone mass per year and is similar to the amount of bone loss that occurs after menopause.

Therefore, it would be wise to avoid an excess of protein in your diet, or you will easily double or triple the rate of calcium — and therefore bone — loss.

Salt and Salt-Restricted Diets: Double Trouble! Table salt is made of sodium chloride crystals. Sodium is an essential nutrient required for maintainence of blood volume, regulation of fluid balance, transport of molecules across cell walls, and transmission of impulses along nerve fibers. Most of us consume ten to twenty times as much sodium as we need or can safely tolerate — which is approximately 1,100 to 3,300 milligrams per day.

You are undoubtedly aware that too much salt is not healthy. It can raise your blood pressure and in so doing increase your risk of hypertension, heart and vascular diseases, and kidney disease. Another health hazard of excess sodium, of which few people are aware, is the risk of losing large amounts of calcium in the urine. This is directly related to quantity: the more sodium in your diet, the more sodium you excrete — and the more sodium you excrete, the more calcium you excrete.

This increase in calcium excretion occurs with no change in the amount of calcium absorbed through the intestine. What probably happens is that as calcium is being excreted in the urine, the blood levels of calcium drop, causing the release of parathyroid hormone, which breaks down bone to restore calcium levels.

It is difficult to say exactly how much salt is too much in terms of its effects on calcium balance. The only study that sheds any light on this question showed that when sodium intake was limited to 200 milligrams per day, there was no change in the amount of calcium excreted, but that at 2,000 milligrams per day there was a significant increase of calcium in the urine. The exact relationship between this calcium loss and bone loss is still not known.

By checking the chart, you will see that 2,000 milligrams of

SODIUM CONTENT OF COMMON FOODS

Food Item	Common Measure	Sodium (mg)	Food Item	Common Measure	Sodium (mg)
Beverages (Alcoholic)			Honeydew	1/5 melon	28
Beer, regular	12-oz can or bottle	18	Orange	1 medium	1
Wine, red domestic	4 fl oz	12	**Meat and Poultry**		
Wine, white domestic	4 fl oz	19	Bacon, regular	2 slices -½ oz	274
Beverages (Nonalcoholic)			Bologna	1 slice	224
Soft drink			Beef, corned	2 slices- 3 oz	802
Regular	8 fl oz	11	Frankfurter, all meat	1 frank- furter	639
Diet	8 fl oz	29	Ham, cured lean	2 slices- 4 oz	1,494
Club soda	8 fl oz	56	Liverwurst		
Tomato juice	6 fl oz	659	(braunschweiger)	1 slice	324
Vegetable juice cocktail	6 fl oz	659	Sausage, pork	1 patty- 2 oz	259
Breads and Crackers			Macaroni with cheese	1 cup	1,086
Biscuit, mix, with milk	1 biscuit	272	Spaghetti, with tomato sauce and cheese	1 cup	955
Bread, white	1 slice	114			
Bread, whole wheat	1 slice	132	**Soups, Commercial Varieties, Condensed (Prepared With Addition of Equal Volumes of Water, Unless Noted)**		
Roll, hard	1 roll	313			
Cereals (Non-Sugar Coated)			Beef broth	1 cup	1,152
Bran flakes (40%)	1 oz-⅔ cup	265	Chicken, cream of (with milk)	1 cup	1,054
Corn flakes	1 oz-1 cup	350	Chicken noodle	1 cup	1,107
Wheat flakes	1 oz-1 cup	370	Onion	1 cup	1,051
			Tomato	1 cup	872
Condiments, Dressings, and Seasonings			**Vegetables (Considered Fresh, Unless Listed Otherwise; Considered Cooked, Unless Indicated as Raw, Sodium Content of Cooked Vegetables is Content Before Salt is Added.)**		
Catsup, tomato	1 tbsp	156			
Salad dressings					
French	1 tbsp	214			
Salt, table	1 tsp	2,325	Asparagus, canned	4 spears	298
Soy sauce	1 tbsp	1,029	Beans, baked, canned, with pork and tomato sauce	½ cup	464
Dairy Products, Eggs, and Margarine			Beans, green, canned	½ cup	319
Cheese, American	1 slice-1 oz	406	Beans, lima, canned	½ cup	228
Cheese, cheddar	1 oz	176	Beets, canned	½ cup	240
Cheese, cottage	½ cup	457	Corn, canned, creamed	½ cup	336
Cheese, parmesan, grated	1 oz	528	Peas, green, canned	½ cup	247
Margarine, soft, tub	1 tbsp	152	Pickles, dill	1 spear	232
Milk, buttermilk	8 fl oz	257	Potatoes, mashed, milk and salt added	1 cup	632
Milk, low-fat (2%)	8 fl oz	122	Sauerkraut	½ cup	777
Fish and Seafood			Spinach, canned	½ cup	455
Crabmeat, canned, drained	1 can- 4 oz	1,250	**Snacks**		
Sardines, drained	1 can- 3¼ oz	598	Corn chips, regular	1 oz	231
Tuna, chunk, canned in oil, drained	1 can- 3¼ oz	328	Nuts, cashews, dry-roasted, salted	4 tbsp- 1 oz	150
Fruits			Potato chips	14 chips- 1 oz	285
Apple	1 medium	2	Pretzels, regular twist	5 pretzels- ½ oz	505
Banana	1 medium	2			

sodium is really not very much. One teaspoon of table salt contains about 2,000 milligrams of sodium, as do 2 tablespoons of soy sauce, two fast-food hamburgers, or 2 cups of canned soup.

Canned, frozen, and otherwise processed foods are loaded with hidden sodium, as are many dairy products. And herein lies the double trouble. Many calcium-rich foods, especially dairy products, are also sodium-rich foods. If you are on a sodium-restricted diet, chances are your calcium intake becomes restricted as well. How can you reduce the sodium in your diet and at the same time maintain a proper calcium intake? First, throw away your salt shaker. Second, avoid those foods high in sodium and low in calcium — the processed foods. And finally, prepare home-cooked meals, as they generally contain less than one-third as much sodium as similar processed foods.

Coffee. Here again we have a situation in which we are not sure how much is "too much." We do know, however, that heavy coffee drinkers lose more calcium from their bodies than non-coffee drinkers. In this regard, Dr. Robert Heany of Creighton University in Omaha, Nebraska, at a recent medical conference commented: "The size of the effect is relatively small but not negligible, and for people who drink lots of coffee every day this could well be a significant factor."

One study has suggested a relationship: in a group of postmenopausal women with reduced amounts of bone, it was found that 31 percent drank four or more cups of coffee per day; in a group of women with normal bone, 19 percent drank that amount of coffee.

Oxalates and Phytates. Oxalates are compounds found in large amounts in green vegetables such as asparagus, beet greens, spinach, sorrel, dandelion greens, and rhubarb. In the intestine, they combine with calcium to form large, insoluble complexes that cannot be absorbed. *Phytates* are phosphorus-containing compounds found principally in the outer husks of cereal grains, especially oatmeal and bran. They, too, interfere with calcium absorption by combining with calcium in the intestine.

It is not necessary to eliminate the above foods from your diet in order to maintain calcium balance. What you should know, however, is that you cannot depend upon them as sources of calcium, nor should you consume your calcium-rich foods (or calcium supplements) at the same time as you eat foods containing oxalates or phytates.

Fiber. Fiber is an important part of your diet. It improves intestinal function, helps promote regularity, lowers choles- terol levels in the blood, improves glucose tolerance, and reduces the risk of colon cancer. Good sources of fiber include bran, whole-wheat breads, brown rice, and fresh fruits and vegetables.

The problem with fiber is that it can prevent calcium from being absorbed. It does this by (1) combining with the calcium in the intestine, and (2) increasing the rate at which food is passed through the intestinal tract. Fiber derived from cereal sources contains phytates, thus limiting even further the amount of calcium that is absorbed.

Fiber is essential, so you don't want to eliminate it from your diet. Just keep in mind that it can limit your calcium absorption; therefore, try not to mix high-fiber foods and those you depend on for your calcium at the same meal. If you are taking calcium supplements, take them either an hour before a meal, about 2 hours after, or at bedtime. And, if you can, try to favor fruit and vegetable fiber over that of cereal origin, which has a higher limiting effect on calcium absorption.

Diets and Fasting. American women are notorious dieters. Fad diets and fasting may be good ways to lose weight quickly (though temporarily), but they are also good ways to lose calcium from your bones.

Most reducing diets are extremely low in calcium and, of course, if you are fasting you are not getting any calcium at all. Since your body requires a certain amount of calcium in the blood to keep your muscles and brain functioning and your blood clotting system in balance, it takes what it needs from your bones. Calcium supplements will enable you to easily meet these needs while still sticking to your diet.

More Bad Press on Stress. Stress decreases the absorption of calcium and increases the amount lost in the urine. Stress also stimulates production of adrenal hormones (which stimulate bone breakdown). Thus, whether you are experiencing emotional stress or physical stress, your need for calcium is increased.

A Warning About Vitamin A. Too much vitamin A can stimulate bone loss. So avoid megadoses — you only need 4,000 international units each day. Daily intakes of more than 5,000 units may stimulate bone loss, according to the American Society for Bone and Mineral Research. Check your vitamin labels, and don't overdo the vitamin A-rich foods: beef liver, carrots, sweet potatoes, apricots, squash, cantaloupe, broccoli, and peaches.

Go Vegetarian!

From the standpoint of your calcium balance and bone health, red meat has more than one strike against it. Because of its acidity and protein content, it promotes the excretion of calcium into the urine. It also contains a good deal of phosphorus, which may predispose you to bone loss. A diet rich in meat is also rich in fat, which is bad from the standpoint of cardiovascular health.

In the light of all this, a shift toward a vegetarian diet may be a good idea. Instead of eating red meat daily, try to have it only a couple of times a week. Since you want to maintain your protein intake, substitute vegetable proteins or "white meat" proteins (fish or poultry) for red meat proteins. In doing so you will not only decrease the phosphorus content and acidity of your diet, you will be eating less fat and more fiber.

Watch Your Calcium-to-Phosphorus Ratio

Until we know exactly what role the ratio of calcium to phosphorus plays in bone loss, it is probably a good idea to try to consume at least as much calcium as you do phosphorus. Because phosphorus is more readily absorbed than calcium, you may want to aim for a calcium-to-phosphorus ratio of 2 to 1.

The easiest way to do this is to avoid excesses of those foods containing large amounts of phosphorus and inconsequential amounts of calcium — red meat, cola drinks, Brewer's yeast (unless supplemented with calcium), and processed foods that contain phosphorus additives. Use the chart of calcium-to-phosphorus ratios of common foods to determine which ones you can easily eliminate from your diet.

CALCIUM, PHOSPHORUS, AND CALCIUM-TO-PHOSPHORUS RATIO OF COMMON FOODS

	Cal (mg)	Phos (mg)	Ratio Ca:P		Cal (mg)	Phos (mg)	Ratio Ca:P
American cheese, 1 slice	188	208	1:1.1	Cheddar cheese, 1 slice	158	100	1:0.6
Apple pie, average slice	9	29	1:2.9	Cherry pie, average slice	17	30	1:1.8
Bacon, cooked, 2 thin slices	1	22	1:22.0	Chicken, fried, 1 drumstick	6	89	1:14.8
Beans, green, canned, 1 cup	81	50	1:0.6	Chicken chow mein without noodles, homemade, 1 cup	58	293	1:5.1
Beef liver, fried, 1 slice	9	405	1:45.0				
Beef noodle soup, canned, 1 cup	7	48	1:6.9	Chicken noodle soup, canned, 1 cup	10	36	1:3.6
Biscuit mix made with milk, 1 biscuit	19	65	1:3.4	Chili con carne with beans, canned, 1 cup	82	321	1:3.0
Bologna, 1 slice	1	17	1:17.0				
Bran flakes with raisins, 1 cup	28	146	1:5.2	Chocolate chip cookies, 4 homemade,	14	40	1:2.9
Broccoli (frozen), boiled, 1 cup	100	104	1:1.0	Chocolate devil's food cake, without icing, 1 cupcake	24	45	1:1.9
Cauliflower (frozen), boiled, 1 cup	31	68	1:2.2				

	Cal (mg)	Phos (mg)	Ratio Ca:P
Coffee, instant, 1 cup	4	7	1:1.8
Corn-on-the-cob, cooked, 1 ear	2	69	1:34.5
Cottage cheese, large curd, 1 cup	212	342	1:1.61
Danish pastry (plain), 1 piece	21	46	1:2.2
Egg, fried, 1 large	28	102	1:3.6
Flounder fillet, baked with butter	23	344	1:15.0
Frankfurter	4	76	1:19.0
French fries, 10 strips	12	87	1:7.3
Ground beef, cooked, 3 ounces	10	196	1:19.6
Ham, baked, 3 ounces	9	201	1:22.3
Hard roll	24	46	1:1.9
Ice cream, plain, soft-serve, 1 cup	253	199	1:0.8
Lamb chops, loin, broiled, 6 9-ounce chops	24	429	1:17.9
Lettuce, shredded, 1 cup	19	14	1:0.7
Lobster Newburg, 1 cup	218	480	1:2.2
Mashed potatoes, with milk, 1 cup	50	103	1:0.8
Milk, whole, 1 cup	288	227	1:2.8
Minestrone soup, canned, 1 cup	37	59	1:1.6
Oatmeal, cooked, 1 cup	22	137	1:6.2
Orange juice, frozen, 6 ounces	19	32	1:1.7
Peanut butter, 1 tablespoon	9	61	1:6.8
Peanuts, roasted, salted	21	114	1:5.4
Peas (frozen), boiled, 1 cup	30	138	1:4.6
Popcorn, with oil and salt	1	19	1:19.0
Pork and Beans, canned, 1 cup	138	235	1:1.7
Pork chops, broiled, 8 2-ounce chops	28	624	1:22.3
Potato chips, 10 chips	8	28	1:3.5
Pretzels, 10 3-ring pretzels	7	39	1:5.6
Puffed rice cereal	3	14	1:4.7
Pumpkin pie, average slice	58	79	1:1.4
Rice, white, cooked, 1 cup	21	57	1:2.7
Rye bread, 1 slice	19	37	1:1.9
Saltines, 10 crackers	6	26	1:4.3
Sesame seeds, hulled, 1 tablespoon	9	47	1:5.2
Shrimp, french fried, 1 ounce	20	54	1:2.7
Spaghetti, homemade, with tomato sauce, meatballs, Parmesan cheese	124	236	1:1.9
Spinach, canned, 1 cup	242	53	1:0.2
T-Bone steak, cooked, yield from 1 pound raw	24	490	1:20.4
Tomato, 1 average	24	49	1:2.0
Tomato soup, canned, 1 cup	15	34	1:2.3
Tuna, canned, 1 cup	13	374	1:28.8
Vegetable beef soup, canned, 1 cup	12	49	1:4.1
White bread, enriched, 1 slice	24	27	1:1.1
Winter squash, baked, 1 cup	57	98	1:1.7

Eliminate All The Secondary Factors You Can

Certain Medications

For many people it is not possible to eliminate such secondary bone-loss stimulators as anticonvulsant drugs, since the risks of withdrawing the medication would far outweigh the potential benefits. Similarly, if you suffer from a disease that causes bone loss, such as kidney disease or Cushing's syndrome, there is nothing you can do. You can, however, together with your physician, reassess your need for those medications that are associated with bone loss.

If you are receiving heparin, is it possible to switch to a coumadin-type anticoagulant? If you are taking a furosemide-type diuretic, can you change to a thiazide type? If you are a frequent user of aluminum-containing antacids, can you cut back on their use and deal with your gastrointestinal problems by dietary and behavior modification? If you have been taking steroids for arthritis, could you achieve similar relief with one of the new, nonsteroidal anti-flammatory drugs? If you are taking more than 3 grams of thyroid hormone, can you reduce your dose?

If you must continue to take these drugs, discuss with your physician what you can do to prevent bone loss. It may be as simple as taking calcium supplements.

Antacids: Some Can Cause Bone Loss, Others Can Help Prevent It. Many of the most popular antacids contain aluminum, which contributes to a negative calcium balance. If you need an antacid, consider switching to one that does not contain aluminum. Some of these contain calcium and can actually be used as calcium supplements. If you are not sure what your antacid contains, look on the label or ask your physician or pharmacist.

Antacids containing aluminum: Amphojel, Delcid, Di-Gel, Gaviscon, Gelusil, Maalox, Mylanta, Riopan, Rolaids, Simeco.

Antacids without aluminum: Alka-Seltzer, Alka-2, Bisodol, Citrocarbonate, Eno, Marblen, Percy Medicine, Titralac, Tums.

Smoking

It has been shown that smoking is associated with an accelerated loss of bone and a greater risk of osteoporosis. If you can't seem to quit, at least cut back, and increase your intake of calcium. It may be reassuring to know that the negative effects on bone appear to be somewhat related to the number of cigarettes smoked. Women who smoked half a pack of cigarettes each day were found to have greater bone mass than women who smoked a whole pack but lessser bone mass than nonsmokers.

Give up this life-threatening habit if you can! At the very least, cut down.

Alcohol

Everyone has a different definition of moderation, especially when it comes to alcohol. In terms of calcium and bone loss, we don't know exactly how much alcohol is too much. We do know, however, that alcoholics are at high risk of osteoporosis. Since drinking is associated with decreased intestinal absorption of calcium, it may be appropriate to avoid drinking any alcohol within 1 or 2 hours of eating your calcium-rich foods or taking your calcium supplements.

Exercise for the Health of It!

What Type of Exercise Should I Do?

Most medical scientists agree that exercise is important for maintaining healthy bones and may, in fact, be the only way to significantly increase your bone mass. Exercise that combines movement, pull, and stress on the long bones of the body is best for the bones. Walking, jogging, bicycling, hiking, rowing, and jumping rope are all excellent. If performed with gusto, these activities can be aerobic exercises, which means your heart, blood vessels, and lungs will also reap the benefits of your efforts.

Although swimming is an excellent aerobic exercise and overall body toner, it is not very effective for preventing bone loss because it does not stress the long bones of the body. For women already experiencing the painful signs of osteoporosis, however, swimming appears to be the exercise of choice, since it allows the benefits of activity without placing undue strain on an already weakened skeleton.

IF SOME EXERCISE IS GOOD, THEN IS A LOT OF EXERCISE BETTER?

Recent research has shown that very strenuous and prolonged physical training in women may actually have a negative effect on bone mass.

Researchers at the University of California School of Medicine studied a small group of young women, some of whom were serious runners, and all of whom had stopped menstruating for no apparent reason. They found that these women had an average bone mass that was 28% below the average for their age!

While the numbers of women studied were small, the results indicate that young women who exercise so strenuously that they stop menstruating may be at risk for bone loss. Because these women have so little fat, they lack normal levels of the type of estrogen that is produced in fat tissue — and this may be why they are losing bone despite the exercise.

More research obviously needs to be done in this area. Most women never get to the point that they stop menstruating because of strenuous exercise. But if you do, it may be a good idea to cut back on your training to a level that does not interfere with menstruation.

How Much Exercise Do I Need?

Unfortunately, we cannot answer with certainty how much exercise is optimal for *skeletal fitness*. Until the results of ongoing research are available, we can only say that it is better to exercise than not to exercise. In the absence of a conclusive guideline, our best recommendation is to exercise for *cardiovascular fitness*. This way, you know you will be meeting one of the primary objectives of exercise and in addition will be helping to prevent bone loss. You will also be controlling your weight, maintaining your flexibility, and toning your muscles.

Exercising for Cardiovascular Fitness

If you follow this program for 6 months you will achieve cardiovascular fitness. To maintain fitness, you must continue exercising for life. Be sure to consult your physician before starting your exercise program, especially if you are unfit, under medical treatment, and/or over 40.

1. Regardless of the type of exercise you choose, whether it is jogging, bicycling, jumping rope, or whatever, you *must* remember to start slowly; begin with at least 5 minutes of warm-up exercises and end with at least the same amount of cool-down exercises. Do your cool-down exercises until your breathing rate and pulse have returned to normal.

2. The name of the game is to exercise to the point that *your heart is working to 70 to 85 percent of its capacity for at least 20 minutes*. To find your maximum heart rate, subtract your age from the number 220. Example: a 35-year-old woman has a maximum heart rate of 185 beats per minute; her 70 to 85 percent target zone is 130 beats per minute (70 percent of 185) to 157 (85 percent of 185).

3. While you are exercising, you need to check your pulse rate periodically to determine when you are in the target zone and how long you stay there. To take your pulse, stop exercising briefly, place two fingers along your carotid artery (at the side of your neck), and count your pulse for 6 seconds. Multiply that

number by ten to determine the beats per minute. If you are below your target zone, keep going and push a little harder. If you are above your target zone, slow down.

4. Maintain your pulse rate in the target zone for 20 minutes, three times a week. Some scientists believe that any more than that will not significantly enhance your performance and may, in fact, increase your risk of injury to joints and muscles.

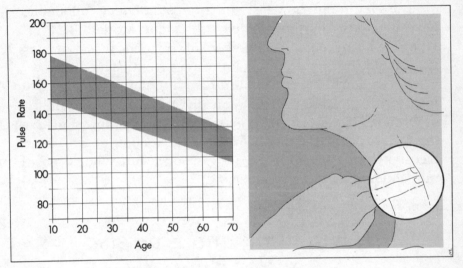

HOW TO FIND YOUR TARGET ZONE

Have Regular Tests for Bone Mass

It is all well and good to follow these recommendations, but if you don't have your bone mass evaluated you will never know how much your efforts are accomplishing. And keeping motivation high without any kind of "progress report" can be difficult.

Ideally, your first bone mass assessment should be done when you are in your 30s or 40s to determine how much bone you have at skeletal maturity. Then, if you find you are entering the bone-losing years with an already low bone mass, you can be particularly careful of your diet and exercise habits and begin controlling as many of the secondary factors (such as smoking and excessive drinking) as you can. If you have a normal amount of bone at skeletal maturity, you are off to a good start, but you still need to watch your diet, exercise, and secondary factors.

Your next assessment should be done at the time of menopause, when the most rapid rate of bone loss begins. In order to determine how fast you are losing bone, you should have at least two or three annual assessments around this time. If you are losing more than 1 percent of your bone mass per year, you should consider stepping up your preventive measures.

After menopause, you should have regular assessments at least until you are 65. How often you need tests will be determined by how rapidly you are losing bone, how sensitive the technique is (the more sensitive the technique, the more frequently tests should be performed), and what type of prevention strategies you are using.

If Nutrition and Exercise Are Not Enough

By following the recommendations given here for preventing bone loss, countless numbers of women will be able to "stand tall," and lead healthy, active lives.

But for some, calcium and exercise are simply not enough. Surgically menopausal women are in this category, as are some naturally menopausal women who have many of the known risk factors for osteoporosis. Also included are the women who just won't follow any regimen, no matter what consequences they may face later. Women who are losing bone rapidly and may need more than calcium and exercise can be identified by testing of bone mass. For all of these women, hormone therapy is the final option, one that can virtually halt bone loss and protect them from the fractures of osteoporosis.

Hormone therapy — its benefits and risks — for women at menopause has long been a controversial issue; although we do not yet have all of the answers, the topic is the subject of much research. Most women know very little about hormone therapy — how it works or how safe it is. Recent advances have shown that hormone therapy can prevent osteoporosis and can also be amazingly safe if used properly by healthy women.

7

Pros and Cons of Estrogen Therapy

Estrogen therapy prevents the bone loss brought on by removal of the ovaries or by a natural menopause. Of all the treatments studied to date, it is the most effective. But, like any drug treatment, it is not without risks.

The Evidence

Ever since 1940 when Dr. Fuller Albright proposed a relationship between estrogen loss at menopause and bone loss, estrogen replacement therapy has been used to prevent or treat postmenopausal osteoporosis. Many of the early studies reported success with estrogens, but they were poorly designed, and so definitive conclusions could not be drawn from them. It was not until 1976, when the first well-designed and controlled study was reported, that it could be said with confidence that estrogen therapy *can* prevent the bone loss that normally follows menopause.

This was a 5-year study of a group of surgically menopausal women, all within 3 years of their menopause. Half the women were given estrogen therapy and the rest received placebos (inactive pills). After only 1 year the two groups displayed significant differences in bone mass. At the end of the 5 years, the placebo group experienced the 1 to 2 percent annual loss of bone mass typical of postmenopausal women, while the estrogen group had *no bone loss at all.* In fact, the women treated with estrogens even gained a small amount of bone.

As a follow-up to this study, the investigators set out to determine how long their patients needed to remain on estrogen therapy in order to prevent bone loss from occurring. They found that if a woman was given estrogen therapy for 4 years and no estrogen therapy for the next 4, she lost just as much bone as a woman who had received no treatment at all! In contrast, the women who received estrogen for the full 8 years showed no bone loss whatsoever.

The Conclusions

A great many studies have confirmed these results and have shown that estrogen therapy is equally effective in preventing bone loss following a natural menopause. From this research, the following conclusions have been drawn regarding estrogen therapy as a means of preventing osteoporosis.

1. The dosage of estrogens required to prevent bone loss is fortunately quite low. As little as 0.625 milligrams conjugated estrogens daily (or its equivalent) has been shown to be effective. This is about *one-third the amount of estrogens contained in the new low-dose oral contraceptives.* No additional protection from fractures is afforded women by

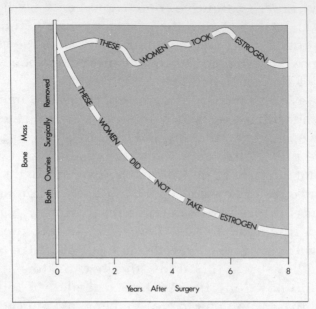

PREVENTION OF BONE LOSS AFTER MENOPAUSE WITH ESTROGEN THERAPY. Women who took estrogen for the first 8 years after menopause did not lose bone. In contrast, women who took placebos lost large amounts of bone.

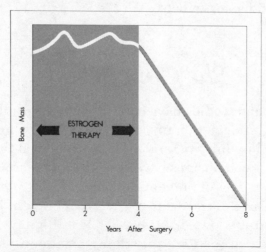

DISCONTINUED ESTROGEN TREATMENT. Women who took estrogen for only 4 years began losing bone as soon as they stopped taking estrogen. After 8 years, they lost just as much bone as women who had received no estrogen therapy at all.

higher doses of estrogens.

2. To be most effective, the therapy must begin within 3 years of the menopause, so as to prevent the large amounts of bone loss that normally occur during this period. Therapy initiated later will still slow the loss, but because some bone has already been lost it cannot prevent fracturing as well as therapy begun earlier.

3. Therapy must be continued until the natural slowing down of bone loss occurs. For most women, this is around age 65 or, usually, 10 to 15 years after a natural menopause. For women whose ovaries have been removed at an early age, the duration of therapy must be correspondingly longer. Although most physicians agree that surgically menopausal women need long-term estrogen therapy, no studies have been made to pinpoint how long it should be.

4. The effectiveness of estrogens as a means of preventing osteoporosis is reflected in their ability to reduce the risk of fractures substantially. Compared with untreated women, *estrogen-treated menopausal women have a 60 percent lower incidence of wrist and hip fractures and a 90 percent lower incidence of vertebral fractures.* Women beginning estrogen therapy within 5 years of their menopause are four times more likely to remain *free* of wrist and hip fractures than women who do not take estrogens.

What the Experts Say

After reviewing all the available evidence, a panel of experts convened by the National Institutes of Health in 1979 reached the following consensus regarding estrogen therapy and osteoporosis:

> *"The group acknowledges the validity of three randomized trials indicating that exogenous estrogens can retard bone loss if given around the time of menopause. Except for dietary calcium, which appears to decrease bone loss to a lesser extent, other substances have not been shown to have such an effect."*

How Do Estrogens Prevent Osteoporosis?

Estrogen therapy after menopause results in an improved calcium balance that protects your bones in the same way that the estrogens produced by your ovaries protect them before menopause.

The estrogens allow calcium to be more efficiently absorbed through the intestines. They also appear to stimulate the thyroid gland to produce calcitonin, which protects the bones from the dissolving effects of parathyroid hormone and inhibits bone breakdown. In addition, estrogens stimulate the liver to produce proteins that bind with the adrenal hormones in the blood and prevent their bone-dissolving effects.

Who Should Take Estrogens?

Estrogen therapy could prevent bone loss in just about every woman after menopause. But because some risk does exist, it would not be medically or ethically desirable for doctors to treat all postmenopausal women with estrogens when only 25 percent will ultimately develop the disorder. The challenge is to identify who is most at risk and recommend therapy to these women before bone loss begins.

It would be ideal if every woman could have her bone mass measured at least twice with one of the sophisticated techniques described in Chapter 5, to find out if she is losing abnormally high amounts of bone. It is possible — even likely — that as public education on this subject grows, and women demand more attention to their health care needs, the future will bring changes. So far, however, few women have access to this equipment, and so your decision to use or not to use estrogens may have to be based on how many risk factors for osteoporosis you have.

The more risk factors you have, the more you stand to gain from therapy. In general, if your ovaries have been removed or if you have had an unusually early menopause, you are at greatest risk and should *strongly* consider estrogen therapy. If you are of small stature, slender build, and fair complexion, you may also be a good candidate for preventive therapy, especially if you have other known risk factors. Daughters, grand-daughters, and sisters of women with osteoporosis should also be urged to consider a preventive program of estrogen therapy.

Who Should Not Take Estrogens?

If you have had cancer of the breast, uterus, or reproductive tract, you definitely *must not* take estrogen — it is absolutely contraindicated. If you have a family history of one of these cancers, you should consider estrogen therapy only if you can be closely supervised.

Several other conditions require an individual assessment of the relative benefits and risks. Diseases involving the liver (where estrogens are metabolized) or the gallbladder can be worsened by estrogens. If you have had blood-clotting disorders, high blood pressure, or heart disease, you should probably avoid estrogen therapy. If you have ever had serious side effects from estrogen therapy or oral contraceptives, you should not take estrogens, although it might be possible if you are checked frequently by your physician. Heavy smokers should not take estrogens; smokers who need estrogen therapy should stop smoking before starting therapy.

The Risk of Cancer of the Uterus

The use of estrogens over a long period of time can overstimulate the endometrium (the lining of the uterus). Without proper treatment this can lead to cancer. Therefore, if your uterus has not been removed and you receive estrogens for long periods of time, you should take a *progestogen* (synthetic equivalent of progesterone) each month to protect the endometrium.

Stimulation of the endometrium is one of the *normal* biological actions of estrogens. *Overstimulation* results when the effects of estrogens are not counterbalanced by the effects of progesterone, as they are during the years of menstruation. Progesterone protects the endometrium by reducing the number of receptors at which estrogens can exert their effects. It also stimulates shedding of the endometrial lining, thus ridding the body of estrogen-stimulated cells before they have a chance to become overstimulated.

When a progestogen is added to the estrogen cycle, the risk of developing endometrial cancer is even lower than it is in women who do not take any hormones at all! A recent study reported that the occurrence of endometrial cancer in estrogen-progestogen users is 0.5 per 1,000 per year, as opposed to 3.8 per 1,000 per year in women receiving estrogen therapy alone, and 1 per 1,000 per year in untreated women.

The risk of developing endometrial cancer is highest among women with estrogen stimulation unopposed by progesterone, whether that estrogen comes from their own ovaries or from estrogen therapy. Therefore, women with anovulatory menstrual cycles (no progesterone production), obese women (estrogen produced in fat from androgens), or women with a family history of the disease are more likely to develop endometrial cancer.

When used alone — not in combination with a progestogen — estrogen therapy can increase the risk of endometrial cancer an estimated four to eight times. While an eightfold increase sounds alarming, it should be placed in proper perspective. The expected incidence of endometrial cancer in untreated women is 1 per 1,000 per year. Even if estrogen therapy increases that incidence to 8 per 1,000 per year, this means that of 1,000 women receiving estrogen therapy, 992 will *not* develop endometrial cancer. To further place these statistics in perspective, remember that women who are 20 percent above ideal body weight have an eightfold greater chance of developing endometrial cancer than women of normal weight.

While the potential risk of endometrial cancer is not to be taken lightly, it is commonly diagnosed in the early and therefore treatable stages. Surgical removal of the uterus (hysterectomy) is the usual treatment. It should be noted that hip fractures are the cause of death in over 40,000 women each year, compared with about 2,300 deaths each year from endometrial cancer — and not all of these are due to estrogen therapy.

Fortunately, adding a progestogen does not interfere with the beneficial effects of estrogens on bone. This has been shown in several investigations, one of which studied a group of

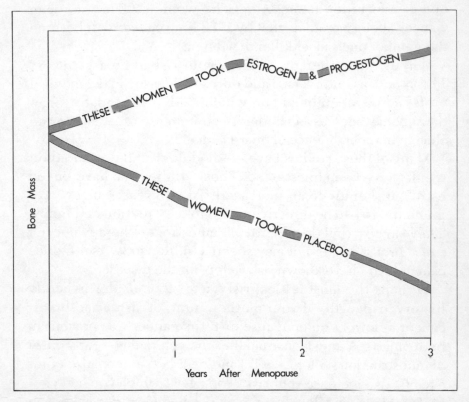

PREVENTION OF BONE LOSS WITH ESTROGEN-PROGESTOGEN THERAPY. In this study of over 300 women, combined estrogen-progestogen therapy preserved the bone mass of women after menopause. Women taking only placebo lost large amounts of bone.

menopausal women receiving both hormones for 10 years. Progestogen therapy alone has been shown to slow down bone loss, although not as effectively as estrogen. In fact, some studies suggest that progestogen may actually stimulate formation of new bone in some women.

The Risk of Breast Cancer

The possibility of developing breast cancer is frightening. This year alone, 110,000 women will have newly diagnosed breast cancers and 37,000 will die from it, making it the number one cancer killer among American women. (The American Cancer Society predicts that by 1983 lung cancer will become the number one cancer killer of women.)

Will estrogen therapy increase your risk of breast cancer? This is both a controversial and unresolved issue in the medical profession. Depending upon which study you read, estrogen therapy has been associated with an increase, decrease, or no change in the incidence of breast cancer.

Many of these studies have methodological flaws, and their results have been questioned. Those studies that have linked estrogen therapy to an increased risk of breast cancer have found the risk to be directly related to the duration of therapy. They suggest (but do not prove) that estrogen therapy doesn't *cause* breast cancer but may speed a hidden growth or induce cancer if you have known risk factors for the disease.

Perhaps the most critical risk factor to consider is family history, especially if your mother, aunt, or sister had breast cancer before her menopause or if the cancer was present in both breasts. A long menstrual life, characterized by early onset of menstruation (before age 12) and/or a late menopause (after age 50) also increase your risk. The age at which you had your first child plays a role: a first pregnancy before age 20 makes you at less risk than a first pregnancy after age 30. Multiple pregnancies seem somewhat protective, as does surgical removal of the ovaries before age 35. Whether or not estrogen therapy after a surgical menopause negates the protective effect of removal of the ovaries is not known.

Evidence is accumulating that the monthly addition of a two week course of progesterone to estrogen therapy can protect the breasts from estrogen stimulation and, just as it protects the endometrium, may actually decrease the risk of breast cancer. These studies are only preliminary, and definitive conclusions must await further research.

Other Potential Risks

Studies of young women who use oral contraceptives suggest that estrogens increase the risk of high blood pressure, thrombosis (blood clots), and cardiovascular disease. However, studies of older, postmenopausal women who receive the relatively safer natural hormones in far lower doses have suggested that these risks may not exist for them. In fact, estrogen therapy after menopause has been found to *decrease* the risk of cardiovascular disease associated with menopause.

On the other hand, if you are obese, smoke cigarettes, have high blood pressure or elevated cholesterol levels in your blood, you are already at risk for these conditions, and estrogen therapy may increase the risk.

Making the Estrogen Decision

How many risk factors for osteoporosis do you have? Have bone mass tests shown that you are losing bone rapidly? Are you already experiencing symptoms of osteoporosis? How many risk factors for endometrial cancer, breast cancer, blood clots, or heart disease do you have? Do you have chronic liver or gallbladder disease? Are you willing to see your physician at least once a year, preferably every 6 months?

You need to ask yourself these questions. Really think them over and *discuss them with your physician*.

If You Decide to Take Estrogens

If you are planning to start an estrogen program to prevent osteoporosis, you will be on therapy for a long time, and there are certain precautions you and your physician must take.

Make sure to have a Pap smear and complete physical, pelvic, and breast examinations *before* you begin therapy. These examinations should be repeated once a year. Check your breasts at home once a month. Have your blood pressure checked every 6 months. If someone other than your physician is checking your blood pressure, be sure to alert your physician if it gets higher.

Your physician may recommend glucose tolerance tests and analysis of cholesterol and other lipids (fats, particularly high-density lipoprotein) in your blood, to be repeated once a year.

If your uterus has not been removed, you need an endometrial biopsy *before* you start therapy and once a year thereafter. A biopsy before you begin taking estrogens is necessary to be certain there are no precancerous cells in the uterus that could be stimulated by the estrogens. Regular biopsies are needed while you are on therapy to make sure the estrogens are not overstimulating the endometrium and increasing your risk of developing cancer.

> *Endometrial Biopsy.* This test is usually done in your physician's office without general anesthesia. A speculum is placed in the vagina to expose the cervix. A small instrument, called a curette, is inserted through the opening of the cervix into the uterus. Samples of the uterine lining are removed for later examination under a microscope.
>
> Some women experience temporary discomfort during an endometrial biopsy which they describe as "like menstrual cramps." Much of this cramping can be prevented by taking one of the new prostaglandin-inhibiting drugs — used for relief of menstrual cramps — before and after the biopsy procedure.

Your physician must prescribe a progestogen for you to take for at least 14 days of every month to protect your uterus. Although this may cause you to have menstrual-like bleeding, which begins each time the progestogen stops, it is an inconvenience most women easily accept when they understand why it is so important. If you bleed at any other time or notice a change in the amount of flow, you must notify your physician at once. To overcome the menstruation "side effect," some physicians are now recommending that low doses of both estrogens and progestogen be given daily without interruption. They claim that menstruation occurs very infrequently and that the uterine lining is well protected.

Even though estrogen therapy will improve your calcium balance, you will still need to pay attention to all those factors that can affect it. While you are on therapy you need at least 1,000 milligrams of calcium and 400 units of vitamin D daily. Watch out for the "bone robbers," and don't forget to exercise!

Types of Estrogen. Conjugated estrogens are the most commonly prescribed estrogen for postmenopausal women. There is no evidence, however, that one type of estrogen product is more effective than another in slowing or preventing bone loss.

Estrogens are usually given orally in tablet form, but they can also be administered by injection or by pellet implantation (under the skin). No studies have been done on the effects of non-oral estrogen on bone mass (although a study of estrogen pellets in surgically menopausal women is now under way at the University of Florida). Below is a list of oral estrogen products your physician may prescribe for you.

ESTINYL *(Schering Corporation)*, ethinyl estradiol

ESTRACE *(Mead Johnson Laboratories)*, micronized 17B-estradiol

ESTROVIS *(Parke, Davis & Company)*, quinestrol

EVEX *(Syntex Laboratories)*, estrone sulfate

OGEN *(Abbott Laboratories)*, estropipate

PREMARIN *(Ayerst Laboratories)*, conjugated estrogens

TACE *(Merrell-Dow Pharmaceuticals)*, chlorotrianisene

If You Decide Not to Take Estrogens

Perhaps you and your physician decide you are not at enough risk of developing osteoporosis to warrant a preventive program of long-term estrogen use. If so, you should at the very least be certain you are getting enough calcium, vitamin D, and exercise. Be alert for signs of osteoporosis — loss of height, rounded shoulders, change in posture, and lower back pain. If these symptoms develop, you and your physician must reassess your need for more aggressive therapy. Ideally, you should be assessed annually for bone loss, using one of the methods outlined in Chapter 5.

8

If You Already Have Osteoporosis

Although osteoporosis may have already caused a certain amount of physical deformity and disability, there are measures you can take to prevent further bone loss, and in so doing you can substantially reduce your chances of more fractures. No treatment can "uncollapse" a collapsed vertebrae, straighten a dowager's hump, or help you regain lost height. But treatment can slow down the bone loss, perhaps even halt it totally, and in some cases actually increase your bone mass.

All women who have had vertebral, wrist, or hip fractures should be treated. "Treatment" is perhaps a misnomer, as osteoporosis is not a disease that can be treated, cured, and forgotten. "Management" is a better term, since therapy must be continued until such time as there is a natural slowing of the bone loss. For many women, this translates into life-long therapy.

How to Keep Your Osteoporosis from Getting Worse

Nutrition

The same nutritional strategies used for prevention are essential ingredients of any management program. You should get at least 1,200 to 1,400 milligrams of calcium and 400 units of vitamin D daily. Because it is important that you absorb as much of this calcium as possible, you need to be especially wary of the "bone robbers" — large amounts of protein, red meat, coffee, salt, fiber, oxalates, and phytates. If you are a smoker, now is the time to stop. This is no time for drinking too much either, as alcohol can prevent you from absorbing the calcium you desperately need and, by causing liver damage, may also impair your body's ability to produce activated vitamin D.

Exercise

If you have never been an exerciser, start now! The secret is to strike a balance between exercise that is beneficial and stimulates new bone formation and overly-strenuous exercise that can actually increase your risk of more fractures. Jogging, for example, is inappropriate for women with osteoporosis, as the jarring motions can traumatize the skeleton.

Daily walking is highly recommended. Because it is not strenuous, you should walk twice a day; once in the morning to limber up and again in the evening. If you are in fair to poor physical condition, researchers at the Brookhaven National Laboratory recommend the following walking program. Begin with a 5-minute walk; preferably in an area with some slopes. Move along at a brisk pace. Add 1 minute each week, gradually building up to a 20-minute walk, brisk and nonstop.

Swimming is another good form of exercise for women with recently established osteoporosis, as it allows the benefits of activity without placing undue strain on an already weakened skelton. As with walking, you should start off slowly, and gradually build up your distance each week.

Your exercise objective is to get to the point of remission or stabilization of the fracture cycle. At this stage — which may occur a year or more following the primary fracture — the exercise program should be gradually upgraded. The amount and type of exercise needed to maximize bone growth is not known. Increasing the muscular support of the weakened skeleton, however, can only be to your advantage. Consult with a physical therapist and develop a personally supervised muscle building program. Your bone was lost a decade or more ago; work *slowly* but *progressively* at building it back up again. You *can* do it!

At the Hospital for Special Surgery in New York City, a special pool for physical therapy is being used for exercising by women with osteoporosis. The water temperature is set exactly at body temperature, 98.6°F, and the water is at breast level. Floats held just beneath the surface support the women as they perform a series of exercises designed to help strengthen their backs.

Dr. Joseph Lane, director of the program, says the same exercises can be done at home in a bathtub, and later, after the fractures are well healed, on the floor or on a hard bed. These exercises should be done for 30 minutes twice a day for the rest of your life.

BACK EXERCISE REGIMEN FOR OSTEOPOROSIS PATIENTS

These exercises should be performed 5 times a week on a firm bed or padded rug. Following *each* movement, relax, lying flat with legs in starting position. Initially each exercise should be performed once, slowly increasing to 5-10 repeats, depending on general capacity and physician recommendations. As limberness increases, the exercises can be supplemented with 50-100 partial sit-ups which should be worked up to slowly.

1. Lie on back with legs bent and bring both knees as close to chest as possible; hold for 5 counts.

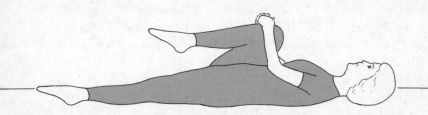

2. Bring one knee to chest while fully extending opposite leg. Hold for 5 counts.

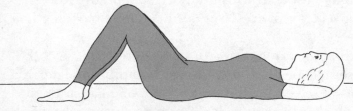

3. Bend knees and keep feet flat; press small of back against surface by tensing buttocks and stomach muscles. Hold for 5 counts.

4. With one leg bent, raise straight leg 6-12 inches off surface, keeping knee straight. Lower leg as slowly as possible.

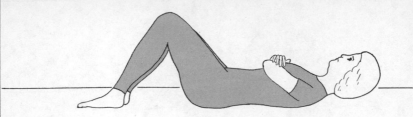

5. Bend knees and place arms across chest; raise head and shoulders. Hold for 3 counts.

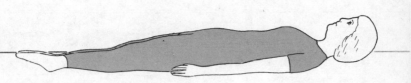

6. Extend legs with arms flat at sides; raise head and shoulders. Hold for 3 counts.

7. Extend both legs and place arms across chest; bring both legs to chest simultaneously. Return to extended position with ankles off surface.

8. Extend legs and place arms across chest; raise legs 6-12 inches. Hold for 3 counts, then lower legs slowly.

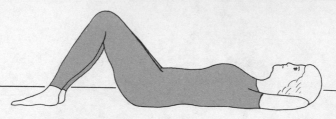

9. Place hands behind neck keeping knees bent; press elbows down to surface. Hold for 5 counts.

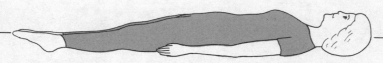

10. Lie on back; squeeze shoulder blades together keeping chin tucked to chest. Hold for 5 counts

11. Lie on stomach with a pillow placed under chest; squeeze shoulder blades together, keeping chin tucked to chest. Hold for for 5 counts.

Drugs in the Management of Osteoporosis: The Choices

Proper nutrition and adequate exercise are the bare requirements for women with osteoporosis. By themselves, they are unable to halt the bone loss process and reduce the risk of new fractures. When used in combination with drug therapy, they can enhance the beneficial effects of the drugs and may in fact reduce the required dosages.

Estrogen and Estrogen-Progestogen Combinations. Estrogen therapy is the most widely studied and accepted means of treating established osteoporosis. If it hasn't been used to prevent bone loss from occurring in the first place, it can at least halt the process of bone loss if it has already begun. Women with osteporosis who take estrogens are relatively protected from further bone loss, height loss, and fractures.

Although definitive studies have not been done to determine the lowest dose of estrogen needed for management, it is generally believed to be greater than that required for prevention. Therefore, if your uterus has not been removed and if you are receiving estrogen therapy for osteoporosis, it is *imperative* that you also receive a monthly course of progestogen to protect the lining of the uterus (and maybe the breasts as well) from overstimulation by estrogen. Since progestogen appears to have the ability to protect the bones from the dissolving action of the adrenal hormones and may actually stimulate the formation of new bone, such a combination regimen can only enhance the benefits of the estrogen therapy.

The same precautions that apply to preventive estrogen therapy apply to management therapy. You need regular physical, pelvic, and breast examinations, Pap smears, blood pressure assessments, and endometrial biopsies.

Anabolic Steroids or Androgens. Recent studies have shown that antabolic steroids or androgens can slow down bone loss in a manner similar to that of estrogens. Investigators have reported that the incidence of adverse side affects (unwanted growth of facial and body hair, acne, and deepening of the voice) can be almost totally eliminated by administering either drug on a "3 weeks on, 1 week off" schedule. Studies of the long-term benefits and risks of anabolic steroids and androgens have not been performed. Until they are, these preparations should be viewed as a viable alternative for women osteoporotics who cannot take estrogens.

Calcitonin. Based on the ability of natural calcitonin to inhibit bone breakdown, women with osteoporosis were treated with injections of synthetic calcitonin. Results were at first encouraging, with small increases in bone mass observed. However, recent follow-up has shown that most patients develop a resistance to the beneficial effects of calcitonin within 1 year, rendering the treatment ineffective. An additional problem with calcitonin is that is must be given by injections. Despite this, the drug is being used in Europe and will soon be promoted here in the United States a treatment for osteoporosis.

Fluoride. Fluoride therapy has received a great deal of recent attention in the press. Of all treatments studied to date, fluoride is the only one that seems able to increase bone mass substantially. Controversy exists, however, as to whether the newly formed bone is normal in composition. Some scientists feel it is too brittle and therefore easily fractured. New data suggest this is not the case and that fluoride therapy may indeed reduce the risk of future fractures.

There are three principal problems with using fluoride for treating osteoporosis: (1) One-third of patients do not respond at all to the treatment; (2) one-third have severe adverse reactions to fluoride, ranging from joint pain and swelling to gastrointestinal bleeding; and (3) the optimal dose of fluoride has not been established. We also do not know for how long people may safely take fluoride therapy; the major investigator has suggested that 5 years may be the limit.

Vitamin D. It was previously thought that large doses of vitamin D were needed to normalize the body's calcium balance. Now we know that excessive amounts of vitamin D — relative to accompanying calcium intake — may stimulate *more* bone loss.

Care must also be exercised if you are taking one of the newly available activated vitamin D preparations. These compounds are synthetic derivatives of the type normally produced by the kidney and are extremely potent. They can, for example, mobilize sufficient calcium to cause kidney stones. Activated vitamin D is not a "routine" method of treating osteoporosis, and if prescribed it must be under the close supervision of a physician knowledgeable in its use. Apart from persons with kidney failure (who are unable to synthesize activated vitamin D), most osteoporotics will probably do as well with the regular vitamin D.

Another new preparation — calcifediol — functions as a partially activated vitamin D, equivalent to the form synthesized by the liver. For total biological action, it needs to be transformed by the kidney into the fully active biological form — activated vitamin D. Toxic side effects are less likely with this compound. Long-term studies documenting the benefit and safety of the "new" vitamin D preparations are not available at present.

What's in the Future?

Unfortunately, no new miracle drug is on the horizon. Future research in the management of established osteoporosis will undoubtedly center around finding which combinations of therapies will halt bone loss and stimulate new bone formation with the least possible risk. Work still needs to be done to identify which therapy is most appropriate for each individual. Ideally, as younger women become aware of osteoporosis and the ease with which it can be prevented, the need for treatment will be lessened.

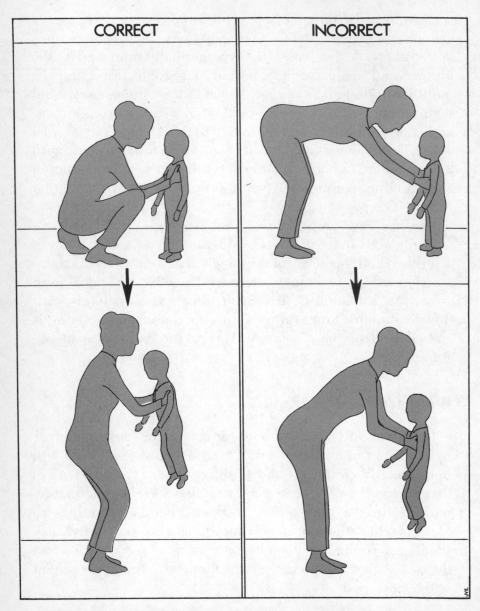

THE PROPER WAY TO LIFT. Use your legs not your back! Bend your knees when lifting heavy objects to avoid back strain and further compression fractures.

9

How to Help Your Daughter Prevent Osteoporosis

The foundation for a healthy skeleton begins in the womb. Protect your own bones and those of your baby by getting enough calcium during pregnancy. (Requirements for calcium during pregnancy are raised by 400 milligrams, to a total of 1,200 milligrams). Try to avoid factors that cause prematurity: an infant born at term increases its bone mineral content by 46 percent within the first 12 weeks of life; infants born 8 to 10 weeks prematurely exhibit only a 12 percent increase.

During your daughter's childhood and adolescence, encourage her to engage in regular exercise. Steer her away from processed and convenience foods and soft drinks high in phosphorus. A nutritious and balanced diet is good bone insurance. In her teens, discourage her from going on crash diets. Avoid the "bone robbers." Discourage her from drinking alcohol and smoking. Remember, the adolescent years are the bone-building years; bone mass increases at a rate of 10 percent per year during this time.

Teach her good nutritional and exercise habits that she will carry into her reproductive years. Oral contraceptives, if not contraindicated for other reasons, will help add bone. Pregnancy, too, may be beneficial to her bones. Even though bone loss in the spine begins in the early 20s, overall bone mass is still increasing until around age 35.

And for both of you: become informed, and find out what resources are available in your community. During the years before and after menopause, be sure to exercise and increase your intake of calcium, and consider switching to a more vegetarian-based diet. Have your bone status checked regularly, if possible, until you are 65.

10

Case Reports

These are actual case histories from the records of the Osteoporosis Screening Program, Center for Climacteric Studies, University of Florida, Gainesville. They are intended to illustrate the multitude of variables that can affect a woman's bone health and to show how each of these is taken into consideration in making recommendations for the individual. Although each of the women described below is different, you may find conditions in their situations that are similar to your own.

The bone mineral content given for each woman has been measured by densitometry, using a single photon absorptiometer.

Women Who Are Not Exhibiting Any Outward Signs of Osteoporosis

Susan

Susan is 35 years old, has very fair skin, is 5'6", and weighs 122 pounds. She has had one full term pregnancy. Because she is adopted she does not know her family history. Susan has epilepsy, for which she takes two types of anticonvulsant medication, and rheumatoid arthritis, for which she regularly takes a nonsteroidal anti-inflammatory agent. She has been on these medications for 10 years. Some time ago she used birth control pills for 6 months.

Susan smokes one pack of cigarettes per day and has done so for 15 years. She drinks six to eight soft drinks per day. She does not drink coffee. Her only liquor consumption consists of about two glasses of wine per week. She does not exercise regularly.

Her daily calcium intake was estimated to be about 600 milligrams, and her daily vitamin D intake was estimated to be less than 100 units.

Bone mineral content: 0.92 grams per centimeter, which is normal for her age.

Comments: Susan has reached bone maturity with a normal amount of cortical bone, despite a number of risk factors: antiseizure medication, smoking, and a high consumption of phosphorus-rich soft drinks. All are capable of interfering with the absorption and metabolism of already compromised calcium and vitamin D intakes. An additional risk factor is her arthritis.

Recommendations: Susan cannot eliminate her antiseizure medication or the arthritis, but she was advised to reduce her *unnecessary* risk factors — cigarettes and soft drinks. In order to compensate for the natural age-related loss of bone she will soon experience, she was encouraged to increase her daily calcium intake, either by diet or supplementation, to 1,000-1,200 milligrams and to increase her vitamin D intake to 400 units per day. She needs regular exercise. Because of her arthritis, which mainly affects her right hip, Susan has to rely on exercises that will not aggravate this condition. We recommended daily swimming to increase and maintain her joint flexibility and a structured weight-training program (such as Nautilus) to strengthen her upper body muscles and the underlying bone. Because of her long-term need for antiseizure medication, Susan is at risk of losing bone at a rapid rate. She was counseled to return regularly for bone density assessments.

Cheryl

Cheryl is 37 years old and has fair skin. She has one child. She has a strong family history of osteoporosis — both her mother and a maternal aunt are affected. She has taken birth control pills for 2 years. She has an ulcer.

Cheryl has a history of extended antacid use. She drinks two to three glasses of wine per week, does not smoke, and does not engage in regular or structured exercise.

Daily intake of calcium was estimated to be 600 milligrams, and daily vitamin D intake was estimated to be 50 units.

Bone mineral content: 0.82 grams per centimeter, which is below the average for her age, indicating that she is in a low bone volume range and may develop a tendency toward spontaneous fractures.

Comments: Cheryl has reached her bone maturity in an already compromised state. The reasons for this may be genetic, since her mother and aunt both have osteoporosis, or they may be related to her use of antacids, her low calcium and vitamin D intakes, or her lack of exercise. Most likely Cheryl's condition was caused by a combination of all these.

Recommendations: There is nothing Cheryl can do about her genetic predisposition. She has been advised to have her gastric problems reassessed and an alternative to antacids prescribed — for example, one of the newer antihistamine drugs that has been found to be effective for ulcers — or to use a non-aluminum-based antacid.

Her calcium and vitamin D intakes must be boosted to the requirement for her age: 1,000 milligrams of calcium and 400 units of vitamin D daily. This creates a problem for Cheryl because calcium supplements stimulate gastric acid secretion, which may aggravate her ulcer. Therefore, we suggested that she take one of the calcium-based antacids (such as Tums). This will soothe her ulcer and increase her calcium intake at the same time. It is especially important that Cheryl take at least one tablet at night, since this is when her ulcer may flare up (because there is no food in her stomach) and most calcium loss occurs.

Cheryl enjoys walking and jogging. To help prevent excessive bone loss, we recommended 20 minutes of jogging, three times a week. Bone mineral assessments will be repeated at 6-month intervals until her rate of bone loss has been established and stabilized. Thereafter, she will be reassessed once a year.

Margaret

Margaret is a 47-year-old redhead with fair skin and freckles. She is 5'4" and weighs 120 pounds. She has four children. She used birth control pills for about 5 years. Her mother developed a dowager's hump at age 80.

Margaret has smoked cigarettes for 27 years and has become a heavy smoker (at least one pack per day) in the last 10 years. She drinks one glass of wine per day and occasionally has two or three cocktails. She drinks three cups of coffee daily and eats red meat at least four times a week. She exercises three or four times per week: Dancercize for 30 minutes and a brisk 1-mile walk. She uses no medication on a regular basis.

Calcium intake (including the small amount of calcium in a daily multivitamin with iron tablet) was estimated to be 680 milligrams per day, and vitamin D intake was estimated to be about 800 units per day.

Bone mineral content: 0.88 grams per centimeter, which is normal for her age.

Comments: Margaret has normal bone density for her age. Her four pregnancies and the use of oral contraceptives may have been important factors, overriding 27 years of smoking. Her mother's osteoporosis developed late in life and in all probability is simply age-related.

Recommendations: Although she is in positive bone balance, (i.e., she has adequate bone stores), we suggested that Margaret reduce her smoking, preferably stopping altogether, and try to reduce her alcohol consumption to one glass of wine or one cocktail per day. Since she is in the premenopausal years, her calcium intake should be increased to at least 1,200 milligrams per day. Her vitamin D intake should be *decreased* to 400 units per day. We also suggested that the amount of red meat she eats be gradually decreased.

Margaret enjoys the companionship of her Dancercize class and walking in the pleasant surroundings of her neighborhood. We encouraged her to continue with both activities and to increase her walking to 2 to 3 miles each day. She will be reassessed in 1 year to determine whether these measures are adequate to prevent her from losing more than the usual amount of bone.

Carol

Carol is 36 years old, 5'3" tall, weighs 125 pounds, and has blond hair and very fair skin. She is the mother of two children. She has taken birth control pills for 4 years and been on thyroid medication for 1 year. Her mother, age 66, has spinal compression fractures, noticeable postural changes, and a recent history of rib fractures.

Carol does not smoke. She drinks two to three glasses of wine per week and eats red meat about twice a week. She walks, jogs or rides a bike three times a week for a total of about 3 miles. Twice a week she participates in a Jazzercize group for 1 hour.

Her calcium intake was estimated to be 800 milligrams per day, and her vitamin D intake was estimated to be 400 units per day.

Bone mineral content: 0.86 grams per centimeter, which is just below average for her age.

Comments: We cannot say for certain why Carol has reached bone maturity with a lowered bone mass. She does, however, have a direct family history of osteoporosis, and she is on thyroid treatment, which is known to increase a woman's risk of excessive bone loss.

Recommendations: Carol has entered her bone-losing phase at a slightly low level. Although at this time she is certainly not at risk of spontaneous fracture, Carol must pay careful attention to those factors that may increase her rate of bone loss from this point on.

She should increase her calcium intake to 1,200 milligrams per day and continue her exercise. We recommended that Carol return on an annual basis so that we can determine her rate of bone loss. If it exceeds 1 percent per year, Carol may become one of the postmenopausal women who will require hormone replacement therapy. Our objective is to have her bones in as good a shape as possible before then.

Anne

Anne is 26 years old, Caucasian, 5'1" tall, and weighs 116 pounds. She is surgically menopausal. At age 22 she had a hysterectomy with oophorectomy (her uterus and both ovaries were removed) because of chronic pelvic infections. Anne has been taking 1.25 milligrams of conjugated estrogens since her surgery. She has never taken birth control pills. She has no children and is not aware of a family history of osteoporosis.

Anne smokes one pack of cigarettes daily and has been doing so for 9 years. She rarely drinks alcohol. She drinks two cups of coffee and one soft drink per day. Her exercise consists of participating in a Jazzercize program twice a week, walking about 20 minutes per day, and riding her bike "frequently."

Her daily calcium and vitamin D intakes are 1,380 milligrams and 590 units, respectively.

Bone mineral content: 0.9 grams per centimeter, which is normal for women of her age.

Comments: Anne's surgery has placed her in a very high risk category for osteoporosis. This exposes her to a dual problem: losing the natural protection of her own estrogens before bone maturity and therefore starting with too little bone, and having an accelerated rate of bone loss. Despite this, her bone mineral content is normal. This is undoubtedly due to the estrogen replacement therapy, although her adequate intake of calcium and vitamin D and her exercise program have certainly helped.

Recommendations: Anne's rate of bone loss will be monitored annually by bone densitometry and blood and urine tests. If these show that she is holding her own, it may be possible to decrease her estrogens dosage by half. We also suggested that a low dose of progestogen be added to her treatment schedule to decrease the possibility of overstimulation of her breast tissue by the estrogens and at the same time have an additive positive effect on her bones. Because Anne's uterus has been removed, overstimulation of the endometrium is not a concern.

Anne will probably need to be on hormone therapy at least until age 50 and perhaps beyond. Because no one knows how long estrogens can protect against bone loss (some say 10 years), it is essential that she continue her exercise program. Until we know exactly what type of exercise and how much is best for preventing bone loss and perhaps even building up new bone, we have advised Anne to participate in one of the more strenuous programs, such as the Nautilus exercises.

Ruby

Ruby is 68 years old, black, 5'7" tall, and weighs 176 pounds. She has one child. At age 36 her uterus and one ovary were removed because of "chronic pelvic pain." She has never taken birth control pills or undergone hormone therapy. She has high blood pressure for which she takes daily medication.

Ruby drinks one cup of coffee per day. Physical activity is limited to a few stretching-type exercises. Her dentist has told her that she has a detectable loss of bone in her lower jaw.

Her calcium intake was estimated to be 525 milligrams per

day, and her vitamin D intake was estimated to be 40 units per day.

Bone mineral content: 0.78 grams per centimeter, which is above normal for her age.

Comments: Ruby has two important features in her favor: she is black and she is overweight. Both are known to be protective against bone loss. Her calcium intake is less than one-third of what it should be, and her vitamin D intake is one-tenth of her daily requirement. In addition, she gets very little exercise. Of note is the loss of bone from her lower jaw; though this could be a sign of early bone loss elsewhere in the body, it may be just a localized dental problem.

Recommendations: Although it is unlikely that Ruby will develop osteoporosis, it must be remembered that her protective features do not make her totally immune. We will therefore monitor her bone density for two more years; if her rate of bone loss is less than 1 percent per year we will feel fairly confident that she will not become osteoporotic, especially as she has already passed through the phase of accelerated bone loss (age 50 to 65).

Nevertheless, we recommended that Ruby increase her calcium intake to 1,400 milligrams per day and her vitamin D to 400 units per day. Because of her blood pressure problem, Ruby must be careful not to increase her sodium along with the calcium (remember that many of the calcium-rich dairy products are relatively rich in sodium as well). For this reason, calcium tablets were recommended. We suggested that she start an exercise walking program that can be gradually increased until she is able to walk 2 miles three times a week. Although obesity is protective of osteoporosis, Ruby should lose about 25 pounds; this, together with exercise, will greatly help to lower her high blood pressure.

Rena

Rena is a 62-year-old white woman who underwent a natural menopause at the age of 48. She is tall and slim and has two children. Aside from some mild arthritis, she is in perfect health. For 10 years she took estrogen but has not received any for the past 4 years.

Rena does daily stretching exercises and walks 6 miles per week. She is a potter and is very active in her trade, bending and lifting a great deal. She has good eating habits.

She gets 1,750 milligrams of calcium per day (all but 100 of these from her diet!) and 600 units of vitamin D.

Bone mineral content: 0.84 grams per centimeter, which is above the average for women of her age.

Comments: Rena is in positive bone balance, certainly as far as her cortical bone is concerned. She exercises regularly, eats properly, and engages in an active occupation. Rena took estrogens for the 10 years when her rate of bone loss was probably increasing. Whether this was responsible for her excellent bone status at this point is speculative, but it does show that estrogen therapy may indeed be most worthwhile for "at-risk" women.

Recommendations: We encouraged Rena to continue her present life-style and to increase her walking to 2 miles per day. We will measure her bone density at annual intervals until age 65 to establish a bone loss pattern. If this pattern is normal, repeat assessments every other year will suffice.

Lilly

Lilly is 57 years old, white, and had a natural menopause 7 years ago. She has been taking estrogens for relief of severe hot flashes and for the prevention of bone loss. She has a strong family history of osteoporosis and used to suffer from arthritis.

Three years ago an endometrial biopsy showed that the lining of Lilly's uterus was being overstimulated. She was therefore given a progestogen to take in addition to the estrogens. Six months later another biopsy indicated that her uterus had returned to normal. Lilly has been on this combined hormone therapy ever since. Because of this she menstruates regularly. She has an endometrial biopsy once a year.

Her calcium intake is 700 milligrams per day, and her vitamin D intake is only 25 units per day.

Bone mineral content: 0.95 grams per centimeter, which is well above the average for women of her age.

Comments: Lilly's case illustrates the importance of careful monitoring during long periods of estrogen therapy. Although the estrogens undoubtedly helped in terms of her bones, they also overstimulated her uterine lining. The latter condition was effectively reversed by adding the progestogen. A consequence is a monthly menstrual period. It is interesting that Lilly's bone mineral content is now *greater* than that of the average for women of her age. With the history of her mother's disabling osteoporosis still clear in her memory, menstruation is for Lilly a small price to pay.

Recommendations: We suggested that Lilly remain on her combined hormone program but increase her daily intake of calcium and vitamin D to 1,000 milligrams and 400 units, respectively. We also recommended that she begin a regular exercise program. Since Lilly likes to ride her bike, we advised she ride several miles three times a week.

Women Who Have Osteoporosis

Diana

Diana is 56 years old, white, and experienced a natural menopause at age 52. She has three established medical problems: osteoporosis (diagnosed by X-ray), high blood pressure, and arthritis. Her osteoporosis is being treated with a daily low dosage of conjugated estrogens (0.3 milligrams).

Diana drinks three cups of coffee and four cups of tea each day. She smokes a pack of cigarettes every day and gets no regular exercise.

Her calcium intake is 412 milligrams per day, and her vitamin

D intake, mainly from supplements, is 22,000 units per day.

Bone mineral content: 0.48 grams per centimeter, which is well below the amount normal for women of her age, placing her at high risk of spontaneous fractures.

Comments: Although she is only 56, Diana already has osteoporosis so severe that the bone loss can be plainly seen on X-rays. This means that she has already lost 30 percent to 40 percent of her bone mass. Her arthritis is a problem commonly associated with osteoporosis and is significant for two reasons: her joint pain may limit much-needed exercise and certain arthritis medications, especially cortisone, may enhance bone loss.

Diana's high blood pressure is an added problem because adequate estrogen therapy may elevate it even further. She is taking a low-dose estrogen for 25 days each month that is probably too low to protect her bones adequately, though it is probably not aggravating her blood pressure either.

Recommendations: Diana has established osteoporosis and needs definitive treatment to slow down her bone loss and, it is hoped, to encourage some new bone growth. Her calcium intake must be increased to 1,400 milligrams per day; the easiest way for her to accomplish this is with calcium supplements. We reminded her to take at least one tablet before she goes to bed at night. Her intake of vitamin D is excessive and must be decreased to 500 units per day (an excess of vitamin D is known to cause bone loss).

The dosage of conjugated estrogens should be increased to 0.625 milligrams in order for it to have any effect on bone. However, Diana was advised to have an endometrial biopsy before the dosage is increased to ascertain if there is any problem in the lining of her uterus that could be stimulated by estrogens. She should also take a progestogen with her estrogens for 14 days each month. This will not only help protect her uterine lining and breasts from the overstimulating effect of the estrogens, it will also help protect her bones. This type of hormone therapy usually results in cyclic bleeding, and we prepared Diana to accept the "side effect" by discussing the importance of the treatment.

Diana was encouraged to stop smoking and to decrease her coffee consumption. She was also shown how to bend down to lift things in a manner that will help avoid further compression fractures. It was suggested that she walk 2 to 3 miles daily. Once her osteoporosis has gone into remission, a more strenuous exercise program can be introduced and supervised.

Diana's bone density will be checked by single photon absorptiometry every 3 months and by dual photon absorptiometry every 6 months until we can determine how well this program is working. Thereafter, she will be tested once a year.

Myra

Myra is 77 years old, has fair skin, a small build, and noticeable transparency of the skin on the back of her hands. She underwent a natural menopause at age 43. She has no children. Nine years ago she had cancer of the lung that was successfully treated with surgery and cobalt therapy. She has had periodontal disease that has required extensive dental work.

Other than the physical activity of her housework, Myra does not get any exercise.

Her daily calcium and vitamin D intakes are 650 milligrams and 100 units, respectively.

Bone mineral content: 0.58 grams per centimeter, which is well below the average for women of her age, placing her at high risk of spontaneous fractures.

Comments: Except for her lowered bone density, Myra is in excellent health for a woman of her age. Her periodontal disease may be related to her osteoporosis, but we cannot be sure.

Recommendations: Myra is at high risk for fracturing her hip. We want to ensure that she can live without the threat of having her life being shortened or of being severely crippled by a hip fracture. We recommended that she supplement her diet with vitamin D-fortified calcium supplements, reminding her to save at least one for bedtime. We encouraged her to begin walking. She is in good physical health, and a daily walk of 2 to 3 miles is well within her cardiovascular abilities.

Her bone density is to be reassessed at 6-month intervals. If we do not see an improvement, we will consider recommending hormone therapy.

Jeanne

Jeanne is 68 years old, white, and underwent a surgical menopause when she was 46. She did not receive estrogens or any other hormone replacement therapy after her surgery. Jeanne complains of constant mid-thoracic back pain, which her physician is treating with androgens. Her spinal X-rays revealed two wedge fractures and five crush fractures of her vertebrae. She has lost 6 inches in height, and she has a strong family history of osteoporosis.

Jeanne has smoked for 40 years and her exercise is limited.

Her daily calcium intake is 1,387 milligrams, and she receives virtually no vitamin D from any source.

Bone mineral content: 0.67 grams per centimeter, which is well below the average for women her age, placing her at high risk of spontaneous fractures.

Comments: We do not know what Jeanne's bone density was at the time of her surgery, so we cannot rule out the possibility that genetic predisposition is the principal cause of her severe osteoporosis. However, failure to receive estrogens after her surgical menopause surely contributed to her present low bone mass.

Nothing can be done to restore the original bone structure of her spine. Therapy must be directed toward stopping further bone loss from her spine, alleviating her backache, and protecting her against an increased chance of hip fracture.

Recommendations: We suggested that Jeanne change to a calcium supplement tablet that contains vitamin D, which she did. She now receives 1,400 milligrams of calcium and 600 units of vitamin D per day.

Because of her chronic back pain, we recommended a bed board under her mattress, exercises to strengthen her back, and a walking program. Because she is in poor physical condition, we advised that the walking program be restricted, but we emphasized the need for her to build up gradually to a 2-mile walk each day.

Although Jeanne is entering the "slowing-down" phase of bone loss, we do not know what her rate of loss is. Until this can be established, we have strongly recommended that she consider taking hormones: we suggested 1.25 milligrams conjugated estrogens daily, to slow down her bone loss and reduce her back pain, combined with a daily low dosage of progestogen to protect her breasts and to slow bone loss as well. If she improves, we will reduce the estrogens to 0.625 milligrams.

Jeanne's bone loss will be assessed at 3-month intervals; once stabilized she will be tested every 6 months; after 2 years she can be "promoted" to an annual assessment.

Claire

Claire is 66 years old, white, and has been surgically menopausal since age 38. She has documented osteoporosis with five vertebral fractures, which have reduced her height from 5′5″ to 4′11″. In addition, Claire has arthritis, angina, an ulcer, and diverticulitis. For the past year she has been receiving 0.625 milligrams of conjugated estrogens daily to arrest bone loss; she also takes medication to decrease her gastric acid secretion and Metamucil twice daily for constipation.

Claire smokes one pack of cigarettes per day. Housework is her only physical activity.

Her daily calcium intake is 1,076 milligrams and she takes special vitamin D supplements totaling over 14,500 units.

Bone mineral content: 0.58 grams per centimeter, which is well below the average 0.78 grams per centimeter for women of her age and places her at high risk of spontaneous fractures.

Comments: Claire has a complicated picture of established

osteoporosis with other conditions whose treatments may interfere with the osteoporosis therapy (it has recently been found that Metamucil interferes with the absorption of estrogens). Thus, the beneficial effect of her hormone treatment is probably negligible. Although Claire's calcium intake is fairly adequate, the amount of calcium actually being absorbed is unknown as she is also on a high-fiber diet for her diverticulitis. Moreover, her vitamin D intake is excessive in relation to her calcium intake and may actually be stimulating bone breakdown.

Recommendations: We suggested that Claire increase her calcium to 1,400 milligrams per day and, because of her high-fiber diet, that she take these supplements between meals, saving at least 500 milligrams to take at night before going to bed. She was instructed to decrease her vitamin D intake to 500 units per day.

Because of the interfering effect of the Metamucil, we advised Claire to have her blood estrogen levels measured to determine just how much estrogen she is actually absorbing. Depending on the result, the estrogens may have to be increased or the Metamucil stopped.

We also recommended that she begin a limited and supervised (because of her angina) exercise program and that she decrease, if not eliminate, cigarette smoking. Claire will be monitored at 3-month intervals.

Helen

Helen is 56 years old, white, and 2 years postmenopausal. She has a strong family history of osteoporosis. She has experienced several fractures of her wrist, all the result of direct trauma. She also suffers from arthritis for which she takes medication. Because Helen has a prolapsed uterus (the supporting structures of the uterus have weakened, causing the uterus to "drop" into the vagina), she has been advised to have a hysterectomy.

Her diet is fairly well-balanced. She walks 1 to 1½ miles each day.

Her calcium intake is 962 milligrams per day and her vitamin D intake is 200 units per day.

Bone mineral content: 0.65 grams per centimeter, which is well below the mean for her age, placing her at high risk of spontaneous fractures.

Comments: We feel that Helen needs estrogen therapy for two reasons. (1) It will enable more of the calcium she takes in to be absorbed and allow less to be excreted, thus helping her reach positive calcium balance. (2) It should slow down her rate of bone loss (remember she is in her maximum loss phase). In order for therapy to be effective, it will probably need to be continued for almost 10 years.

Recommendations: We advised Helen to have the hysterectomy her physician recommended. Not only will this relieve the distressing symptoms of her uterine prolapse, but it will remove any worry about estrogens overstimulating her endometrium. (However, a hysterectomy should never be performed simply to allow the patient to take hormones without the need for endometrial biopsies or the inconvenience of possible menstruation.) We recommended hormone therapy and asked Helen to boost her calcium intake to 1,200-1,400 milligrams per day and her vitamin D to 400 units.

Faye

Faye is a petite 58-year-old oriental woman from Malaysia. She has three children. She has been on treatment with estrogen pellets and a progestogen for the past 15 years.

She is an active woman, who gardens extensively and plays tennis three times a week.

Her daily calcium intake is only 345 milligrams, and her daily vitamin D intake is only 75 units.

Bone mineral content: First assessment — 0.77 grams per centimeter, below the average for her age. Six months later — 0.80 grams per centimeter at the identical plane of previous measurement. Within the limits of error of the instrument used, this is equivalent to 6.5 percent bone gain per year.

Comments: When Faye first came in for assessment she was taking adequate hormone replacement, but her diet was markedly deficient in calcium and vitamin D.

Recommendations: We suggested that Faye continue the hormones and increase her daily calcium and vitamin D intakes to 1,000 milligrams and 400 units, respectively. How much of the increase seen after only 6 months could be attributed to the calcium and vitamin D increase cannot be determined. Nevertheless, her example illustrates two points. (1) Estrogen therapy alone cannot prevent osteoporosis; adequate amounts of calcium and vitamin D are necessary in the diet. (2) Oriental women, despite their genetically-based high risk of osteoporosis, can be assured good bone mineral content by appropriate therapy.

Connie

Connie is a petite 52-year-old Vietnamese who underwent a natural menopause at age 45. She has three children. Aside from a lower backache, she has no major health problems. A recent spinal X-ray revealed that Connie has at least one crush fracture in the lower back area.

Connie does some fairly strenuous work in a restaurant but gets no regular or structured exercise.

Her calcium intake is only 250 milligrams per day, and her vitamin D intake is negligible.

Bone mineral content: 0.53 grams per centimeter, which is well below the average for her age, placing her at high risk of spontaneous fractures.

Comments: Oriental women are especially prone to osteoporosis. It is unclear just how much of this tendency is genetic and how much is environmental. In Connie's case, it may be that a lifelong calcium deficient diet with superimposed pregnancies contributed to her advanced state of bone loss. In addition, Connie has just experienced the most accelerated phase of her anticipated postmenopausal bone loss pattern.

Recommendations: Connie's daily calcium and vitamin D intake were stepped up to the requirements for her age and menopausal status — 1,400 milligrams and 400 units, respectively. We recommended that she begin an estrogen-progestogen regimen and a regular exercise program of walking and bicycling. She will return every 3 months for reassessment to see how well this program is working for her.

Marian

Marian is 53 years old, white, and 3 years postmenopausal. She has a family history of osteoporosis but no other significant health features.

Marian drinks 4 to 6 ounces of alcohol per day and has done so for the past 20 to 25 years. She does calisthenic-type exercises for about 10 minutes daily and plays golf regularly.

Her calcium intake is 625 milligrams per day, and she gets regular sun exposure but virtually no vitamin D from her diet.

Bone mineral content: First assessment — 0.79 grams per centimeter, which is below the average for her age, meaning that she was developing a tendency toward spontaneous fractures. Six months later — 0.74 grams per centimeter, a loss (within the limitations of our instrument) equivalent to 9.4 percent per year.

Comments: When Marian first came for assessment she was advised to increase her calcium and vitamin D intakes and reduce her alcohol consumption. During the 6-month period between her bone mineral content measurements, she increased her calcium and vitamin D intakes marginally to 850 milligrams and 150 units per day, respectively, but was unable to curtail her alcohol intake.

Recommendations: We stressed the importance of adequate calcium and vitamin D to her and suggested that she begin using calcium supplements since it had been so hard for her to get all she needed from her diet alone. She was reminded to take at least one-third of her daily supplements at bedtime. We also explained that too much alcohol can compromise calcium balance. Although we still do not know how much is too much, in Marian's case, 4 to 6 ounces is probably too much. As for exercise, we advised Marian to walk her 18 holes of golf instead of riding in a cart!

Because her rate of bone loss appears to be rapid and because she seems unable to slow it down with dietary and exercise strategies, we suggested that she discuss the use of hormone therapy with her physician. In either case, she will be monitored at 3-month intervals. Only with a number of repeated measurements will we be able to definitely plot her rate of bone loss and determine her treatment needs.

Doreen

Doreen is a 47-year-old black woman. Earlier this year she had a total hysterectomy, with removal of both ovaries because of a fibroid tumor in her uterus. She has had six pregnancies and now has five living children.

On assessment of her dietary intake, she was found to have a very low daily consumption of both calcium and vitamin D, 445 milligrams and 100 units respectively. This diet is reflective of lifelong food habits.

Bone mineral content: 0.45 grams per centimeter, which is well below the average for women of her age, placing her at high risk of spontaneous fractures

Comments: Black women *can* be bone deficient. If calcium intake is sufficient, multiple pregnancies are protective of bone and can actually increase bone mass. When intake is deficient the reverse is true. This may, in fact, explain Doreen's low bone mass.

Although we don't know what Doreen's bone mass was before her ovaries were removed, we do know that she would have had at least three more years of natural estrogen protection for her bones. In retrospect, it may have been wise if Doreen's physician had not removed her ovaries when the hysterectomy was performed.

Recommendations: Doreen was advised to supplement her diet with calcium and vitamin D and was put on estrogens and progesterone hormone treatment. She was also encouraged to begin a daily exercise program of walking.

Her bone mineral content will be reassessed at 6-month intervals until we are able to establish her pattern of bone loss.

Grace

Grace is 26 years old, white, and has never menstruated. She has been informed that her ovaries are nonfunctioning. She has a normal uterus and is otherwise in good health. She has never received hormone therapy.

Grace does calisthentics for 5 to 10 minutes each day and swims seasonally.

Her intake of calcium and vitamin D is grossly inadequate — only 360 milligrams and 43 units daily, respectively.

Bone mineral content: 0.81 grams per centimeter, which is below the average for her age, meaning that she might be developing a tendency toward spontaneous fractures.

Comments: Although Grace's ovaries have not been removed, her case illustrates the accelerated bone loss and premature osteoporosis that occurs as a consequence of having the ovaries removed before menopause without receiving any hormone therapy; it occurs in 50 percent of the women in this situation. It must be remembered that Grace is only 26 years old and already has low levels of cortical bone; in all probability her trabecular bone level (not measured) is even lower.

Recommendations: Grace needs to receive estrogens and progesterone: estrogens to slow down her bone loss and progesterone to protect the breasts and the lining of the uterus from estrogen overstimulation.

She has been told that she will need annual endometrial biopsies (to check on the uterine lining) for 3 years; if negative, they can then be done every other year and eventually every 3 years. She has been instructed in breast self-examination. She will have a mammography (to get a good baseline picture of her breast structure) soon, and it will be repeated every 3 years. Her bone mineral content will be assessed every 6 months for at least 2 years and then annually until it is clear that the therapy is working.

11

Planning a Healthy Future

Osteoporosis is one of the most significant health hazards to the older women in this country. Women and their health-care professionals should direct their efforts at prevention, since bone, once lost, cannot be restored. Ignorance of osteoporosis, its ramifications, and its prevention can be very dangerous.

For many women, menopause comes at a time when life's achievements and goals are being reassessed. The middle years are often a period of contemplating the past and planning the future.

Just as you plan for the financial, social, and emotional security of your later years, so, too, you should plan for your physical health. Paying attention to good nutrition, getting plenty of exercise, and maybe taking hormones will make you feel better now and will keep you healthier for your later years. To fully enjoy your expected 28 years after menopause, you need to be healthy!

The time to start preventing bone loss is now, before it begins. It's never too early, but it can be too late.

Glossary

ACUTE PHASE. The time immediately following fracture of a spinal vertebra, characterized by sharp pain at the level of the fracture. This phase usually lasts from 1 to 4 weeks and is followed by the dull muscle ache of the chronic phase.

ADRENAL GLANDS. Small, pyramid-shaped glands situated atop the kidneys.

ADRENAL HORMONES. The substances manufactured and released by the adrenal glands. Some of these hormones are harmful to bone.

ADRENOPAUSE. The time, usually around age 65, when the production of some of the adrenal hormones slows down.

ALKALINE PHOSPHATASE. A liver enzyme involved in calcium metabolism.

AMINO ACIDS. Organic compounds that are the primary components (building blocks) of proteins.

ANABOLIC STEROIDS. Hormones that stimulate tissue growth; they are similar to the androgens.

ANDROGENS. The hormones responsible for the development and maintenance of male sex characteristics and reproductive function in men. Androgens are produced by the testes and adrenal glands in men and in small amounts by the adrenal glands in women.

ANGINA. A spasmodic choking or suffocating pain in the chest.

ANTACIDS. Preparations used to counteract overacidity in the stomach.

ANTICONVULSANTS. Drugs used to control seizures as in epilepsy.

BICONCAVE. Having a depressed, or hollowed-out surface on both the front and back sides.

BONE MASS. The total amount of bone in the body. Overall bone mass increases from birth and reaches a peak around the age of 30. Thereafter, it declines as bone is lost with age.

BONE MINERALIZATION. The last step in the formation of new bone when calcium and phosphorus crystals fill in the collagen matrix.

BONE REMODELING. The cyclic process of bone breakdown and formation that is responsible for growth, maintenance, and repair of bone tissue.

CALCITONIN. A "calcium-sparing" hormone released primarily by the thyroid gland. It acts to slow down the breakdown of bone.

CALCIUM. A metallic element found in nearly all living tissues. It gives bone most of its structural properties (99% of the body's calcium is in the bones) and is required for muscle contraction, blood clotting, and nerve impluse transmission.

CALCIUM BALANCE. The net of the processes in which calcium enters the body (through the diet) and leaves the body (through the sweat, urine, and feces). A *negative calcium balance* means that more calcium is being excreted than is being taken in (the extra calcium comes from the bones). A *positive calcium balance* means that more calcium is being taken in than is being excreted.

CALCIUM "THERMOSTAT." The regulating mechanism involving parathyroid hormone, vitamine D, and calcitonin that maintains a relatively constant level of calcium in the blood.

CALCIUM-TO-PHOSPHORUS RATIO. The amount of calcium in the diet relative to the amount of phosphorus in the diet.

CALIPERS. Instrument with two bent or curved legs that can be adjusted to make fine measurements of thickness or width.

CAT (COMPUTERIZED AXIAL TOMOGRAPHY) SCAN. A method of viewing cross sections of tissue or bone with X-rays.

CERVIX. The narrow lower end of the uterus which extends into the vagina (Pap smears are taken from the cervix).

CHRONIC PHASE. The time following the acute phase of a spinal vertebral fracture. It is characterized by a dull muscle ache in the mid or lower back.

CODFISHING. The beginning of the collapse of two spinal vertebrae at which time the space between them takes on a fish-shaped appearance.

COLLAGEN. The protein that is the supportive component of bone, connective tissue, cartilage, and skin.

COLLE'S FRACTURE. A break of the lower part of the radius; it is commonly called a wrist fracture.

CORTICAL BONE. The hard dense bone that forms the outer shell of all bones.

CORTICOSTEROIDS. Drugs that resemble the adrenal hormones; they are sometimes used to treat asthma or arthritis.

CORTISONE. An adrenal hormone which can be harmful to bone. It also refers to a drug resembling the adrenal hormone.

CRUSH FRACTURE. A spinal vertebral break in which both the front and back sections have collapsed.

CURETTE. A small instrument used to scrape bits of tissue from the lining of the uterus for later inspection under a microscope.

CUSHING'S SYNDROME. Overactivity of the adrenal glands.

DENSITOMETER. An instrument that measures the density of bones by determining the amount of radiation they can absorb.

DIABETES. A disease that impairs the body's ability to use sugar.

DIURETICS. Drugs that promote the excretion of urine.

DIVERTICULITIS. Inflammation of a part of the intestines; usually causes crampy pain in the lower left side of the abdomen.

DOWAGER'S HUMP. A protruberance of the upper back caused by painful collapsing of the vertebrae and outward curvature of the upper spine.

DUAL PHOTON ABSORPTIOMETRY. A sensitive method of measuring the amount of trabecular bone in the spine.

ENDOMETRIAL BIOPSY. The procedure of removing a sample of the lining of the uterus for testing.

ENDOMETRIAL CANCER. Cancer of the lining of the uterus.

ENDOMETRIOSIS. A sometimes painful condition in which pieces of the endometrial tissue are found outside the uterus attached to the surface of the uterus, ovaries, tubes, or rectum.

ENDOMETRIUM. The lining of the uterus.

ENVELOPES. The lining, outer, and "in between" surfaces of bone. The *periosteal envelope* is the outer surface, the *endosteal envelope* is the inner surface that lines the bone marrow cavity, and the *intracortical envelope* is the area between the two.

ESTROGENS. The hormones responsible for the development and maintenance of female sex characteristics and reproductive function in women. Estrogens are produced by the ovaries in women and in small amounts by the testes in men. Laboratory-produced estrogens can be administered to women to correct hormonal problems.

FEMUR. The thigh bone (the longest and strongest bone in the body).

FLUORIDE. A chemical element that promotes formation and growth of teeth and bones. It is sometimes added to community water supplies to prevent dental cavities and is being used as an experimental treatment of osteoporosis.

FRATERNAL TWINS. Twins that develop from separate fertilized eggs.

GROWTH HORMONE. A substance produced by the pituitary gland that stimulates growth in many tissues throughout the body.

HORMONE. A chemical substance produced in one part of the body and carried in the blood to another part of the body where it has specific effects.

HORMONE REPLACEMENT THERAPY. Treatment to restore hormones lost by removal of the ovaries (as after a surgical menopause) or to correct a hormonal imbalance or deficiency (as can occur after a natural menopause).

HYPERPARATHYROIDISM. Overactivity of the parathyroid glands.

HYPERTENSION. High blood pressure.

HYPERTHYROIDISM. Overactivity of the thyroid glands.

HYSTERECTOMY. Surgical removal of the uterus. A *total* or *complete hysterectomy* refers to surgical removal of both the uterus and cervix.

IDENTICAL TWINS. Twins that develop from a single fertilized egg.

KYPHOSIS. Outward curvature of the upper spine.

LACTASE. An intestinal enzyme that breaks down lactose, a sugar, into small, easily digested components.

LACTASE DEFICIENCY. A deficiency of the enzyme lactase resulting in uncomfortable gastrointestinal symptoms when foods containing lactose are eaten. (Also called *lactose intolerance.)*

LACTOSE. A sugar found in milk and other dairy products.

LORDOSIS. Inward curvature of the lower spine.

LUMBAR VERTEBRAE. The bones of the spinal column in the lower part of the back.

METACARPALS. The bones of the hand between the wrist and fingers.

NATURAL MENOPAUSE. A developmental phase characterized by decreased estrogen and progesterone production, the end of menstruation, and loss of child-bearing potential. For most women, menopause occurs around the age of 50.

OOPHORECTOMY. Surgical removal of the ovaries.

OPAQUE SKIN. Skin of normal thickness.

OSTEOBLASTS. Small cells that fill in the cavities dug by the osteoclasts and produce the collagen matrix of new bone.

OSTEOCLASTS. Large cells that initiate the bone remodeling cycle by "digging" cavities in existing bone tissue.

OSTEOMALACIA. A bone disease in adults caused by vitamin D deficiency and characterized by inadequate mineralization of new bone.

OSTEOPENIA. A reduction in overall bone mass to a level below "normal" but still above that associated with fracturing.

OSTEOPOROSIS. A reduction in overall bone mass (characterized by increased porosity and thinning of the bones) to the point that microscopic or more obvious fracturing has occurred. *Primary osteoporosis* cannot be traced to one single cause and is usually the result of interaction among genetic, nutritional, and environmental factors. *Secondary osteoporosis* is usually the result of a drug or disease which causes bone loss. *Postmenopausal osteoporosis* occurs in 25 percent of women after a natural menopause and in 50 percent of women not receiving hormone replacement therapy after a surgical menopause. It is directly related to the loss of estrogens and progesterone and also to interactions among genetic, nutritional, and environmental factors. *Disuse osteoporosis* is caused by prolonged immobilization, bed rest, paralysis, or weightlessness.

OXALATES. Compounds that can interfere with the absorption of calcium. They are found in some leafy green vegetables.

PARATHYROID GLAND. Four tiny organs near the thyroid gland (two on each side) in the neck.

PARATHYROID HORMONE. A substance released by the parathyroid glands in response to low levels of calcium in the blood. It stimulates the breakdown of bone in order to release calcium and restore normal levels in the blood.

PELVIC INFLAMMATORY DISEASE. A bacterial infection of the lower pelvic region.

PERIODONTAL DISEASE. An inflammation of the sockets of the teeth; it leads to loosening and sometimes loss of teeth.

PHOSPHORUS. A nonmetallic element found in all living tissues and involved in almost every metabolic process. Together with calcium it provides much of the structural framework of bones.

PHYTATES. Phosphorus-containing compounds that can interfere with the absorption of calcium. They are found in the outer husk of cereal grains.

PITUITARY GLAND. A small oval organ at the base of the brain; it produces many important hormones and has been called the "master gland."

PLACEBO. An inactive substance, frequently in the form of a pill, used in controlled scientific studies to determine the effectiveness of drugs.

PLAQUE. A buildup of material on the teeth that can foster bacterial growth.

PROGESTERONE. The hormone produced by the ovary during the second half of the menstrual cycle. It acts to prepare the uterus for pregnancy.

PROGESTOGEN. A synthetic preparation that resembles the natural hormone progesterone.

PYORRHEA. A term sometimes used as a synonym for periodontal disease.

RADIOGRAMMETRY. A method of measuring the thickness of the outer cortical shell of bones on X-rays.

RADIOGRAPHIC PHOTODENSITOMETRY. A method of measuring the density of bones on X-rays.

RADIUS. The smaller and shorter of the two bones of the forearm.

RECEPTOR. A tiny area on the surface of cells or membranes at which specific substances "fit" (like a lock and key) and exert their effects.

REMISSION. The time after a spinal vertebral fracture following the acute and chronic phases during which symptoms and pain have abated.

RESORPTION. The process of bone breakdown in the bone remodeling process.

RHEUMATOID ARTHRITIS. A chronic inflammatory disease of the joints.

RICKETS. A bone disease of infants and young children caused by vitamin D deficiency and resulting in defective bone growth.

SINGLE PHOTON ABSORPTIOMETRY. A sensitive method of measuring the density of bone in the long bones of the body, usually the arm.

SURGICAL MENOPAUSE. A premature menopause brought on by surgical removal of the ovaries before the woman has experienced a natural menopause.

THORACIC VERTEBRAE. The bones of the spinal column in the area of the middle of the back.

THYROID GLAND. An organ at the base of the neck primarily responsible for regulating the rate of metabolism.

THYROID HORMONES. Substances released by the thyroid gland which regulate metabolism. Excessive amounts can cause bone loss.

TRABECULAR BONE. The porous, spongy bone that lines the bone marrow cavity and is surrounded by cortical bone.

TRANSPARENT SKIN. Thin, unpigmented skin through which the fine details of the underlying veins can be seen.

ULNA. The inner and larger bone of the forearm.

UTERUS. The womb.

VITAMIN D. Considered to be both a vitamin and a hormone, vitamin D is produced in the skin during sun exposure and is available from several foods. In the body, vitamin D is one of the three hormones of the calcium "thermostat." Normal levels are beneficial to bone and promote calcium absorption and limit calcium excretion. High levels can cause bone loss.

WEDGE FRACTURE. A spinal vertebral break in which the front but not the back section of the vertebra has collapsed.

Bibliography

Chapter 1.   Your Bones and How They Change

Frost, H. M. *Bone remodeling and its relationship to metabolic bone diseases.* Springfield, Illinois: Charles C. Thomas, 1973.

Frost, H. M., Tetracycline-based histological analysis of bone remodeling. *Calcified Tissue Research* 3: 211, 1969.

Gain, S. M. The phenomena of bone formation and bone loss. In *Osteoporosis. Recent advances in pathogenesis and treatment,* eds. H. F. Deluca, et al. Baltimore, Maryland: University Park Press, 1981.

Mazess, R. B. On aging bone loss. *Clinical Orthopaedics and Related Research* 165: 239, 1982.

Recker, R. R. *Postmenopausal osteoporosis. Causes, diagnosis, and treatment.* New York: Ayerst Laboratories, May 1980.

Riggs, B. L., et al. Differential changes in bone mineral density of the appendicular and axial skeleton with aging. *Journal of Clinical Investigation* 67: 328, 1981.

Chapter 2.   Understanding the Problem

Aaron, F. E., et al. Osteomalacia and osteoporosis in fractures of the proximal femur. *Lancet* 1: 299, 1974.

Gallagher, J. C., et al. Epidemiology of fractures of the proximal femur in Rochester, Minnesota. *Clinical Orthopaedics and Related Research* 149: 207, 1980.

Gordan, G. S., et al. Early detection of osteoporosis and prevention of hip fractures in elderly women. *Medical Times* 109: 1s, 1982.

Horsman, A., et al. Cortical and trabecular osteoporosis and their relation to fractures in the elderly. In *Osteoporosis. Recent advances in pathogenesis and treatment,* eds. H. F. DeLuca, et al. Baltimore, Maryland: University Park Press, 1981.

Iskrant, A. P. The etiology of fractured hips in females. *American Journal of Public Health* 58: 485, 1968.

Keene, J. S., and Anderson, C. A. Hip fractures in the elderly. Discharge predictions with a functional rating scale. *Journal of the American Medical Association* 248: 564, 1982.

Knowelden, J., et al. Incidence of fractures in persons over 35 years of age. *British Journal of Preventive and Social Medicine* 18: 130, 1974.

McKenzie, L., and Notelovitz, M. Osteoporosis-related fractures of the femur: The financial cost. Submitted for publication, 1982.
Miller, C. W. Survival and ambulation following hip fracture. *Journal of Bone and Joint Surgery* 60A: 930, 1978.

Newton-John, H. F., et al. The loss of bone with age, osteoporosis and fractures. *Clinical Orthopaedics and Related Research* 71: 299, 1970.

Owen, R. A., et al. The national cost of acute care of hip fractures associated with osteoporosis. *Clinical Orthopaedics and Related Research* 150: 172, 1980.

Parfitt, A. M., and Duncan, H. Metabolic bone disease affecting the spine. In *The spine,* ed. F. Simeone. Philadelphia, Pennsylvania: W. B. Saunders, 1975.

Stewart, I. M. Fractures of the neck and femur: survival and contralateral fracture. *British Medical Journal* 2: 922, 1957.

Chapter 3.   How Your Body Regulates Bone Mass

Atkins, D., et al. The effect of oestrogens in the response to bone to parathyroid hormone in vitro. *Journal of Endocrinology* 54: 107, 1972.

Chen, T. L., and Feldman, D. Distinction between alpha-fetoprotein and intracellular estrogen receptors. Evidence against the presence of estradiol receptors in rat bone. *Endocrinology* 102: 236, 1978.

Chen, T. L., et al. Glucocorticoid receptors and inhibition of bone cell growth in primary culture. *Endocrinology* 100: 619, 1977.

Gallagher, J. C., et al. Intestinal calcium and serum vitamin D metabolites in normal subjects and osteoporotic patients. Effect of age and dietary calcium. *Journal of Clinical Investigation* 64: 729, 1979.

Heath, H., and Sizemore, G. W.   Plasma calcitonin in normal man. *Journal of Clinical Investigation* 60: 1135, 1977.

Meema, S., and Meema, H. E. Menopausal bone loss and estrogen replacement. *Israel Journal of Medical Sciences* 12: 9, 1976.

Milhaud, G., et al. Deficiency of calcitonin in age-related osteoporosis. *Biomedicine* 29: 272, 1978.

Orimo, H., et al. Increased sensitivity of bone to parathyroid hormone in ovariectomized rats. *Endocrinology* 90:760, 1972.

Rico, H., et al. The role of growth hormone in the pathogenesis of postmenopausal osteoporosis. *Archives of Internal Medicine* 139: 1263, 1979.

Shamonki, I. M., et al. Age-related changes of calcitonin secretion in females. *Journal of Clinical Endocrinology and Metabolism* 50: 437, 1980.

Stevenson, J. C., et al. Calcitonin and the calcium-regulating hormones in postmenopausal women: Effect of oestrogens. *Lancet* 1: 693, 1981.

Tanaka, Y., et al. Sex hormone control of the renal vitamin D hydroxylases. In *Vitamin D: Biochemical, chemical and clinical aspects related to calcium metabolism,* eds. A. W. Norman, et al. New York: Walter de Groyter, 1977.

Chapter 4.   Will You Get Osteoporosis?

Aloia, J. F., et al. Prevention of involutional bone loss by exercise. *Annals of Internal Medicine* 89: 356, 1978.

Aloia, J. F., et al. Skeletal mass and body composition in marathon runners. *Metabolism* 27: 1793, 1978.

Bernstein, D. S., et al. Prevalence of osteoporosis in high- and low-fluoride areas in North Dakota. *Journal of the American Medical Association* 198: 499, 1966.

Bones in space. Editorial. *British Medical Journal* 1: 1288, 1980.
Brighton, C. T., et al. *Electrical properties of bone and cartilage.* New York: Grune & Stratton, 1979.

Chastain, G. C. Urinary calcium excretion in noninstitutionalized elderly as related to sex, race, diet, body size and activity. Master's thesis, Auburn University, Auburn, Alabama, 1982.

Cornil, A., et al. Effect of muscular exercise on the plasma level of cortisol in man. *Acta Endocrinologica* 48: 163, 1965.

Daniell, H. W., Osteoporosis and smoking. *Journal of the American Medical Association* 221: 509, 1972.

Daniell, H. W. Osteoporosis of the slender smoker. Vertebral compression fractures and loss of metacarpal cortex in relation to postmenopausal cigarette smoking and lack of obesity. *Archives of Internal Medicine* 136: 298, 1976.

Dequeker, J., et al. The effect of long-term lynestrenol treatment on bone mass in cycling women. *Contraception* 15: 715, 1977.

Dicker, R. C., et al. Hysterectomy among women of reproductive age. Trends in the United States, 1970-1978. *Journal of the American Medical Association* 248: 323, 1982.

Doyle, F. H., et al. Relation between bone mass and muscle weight. *Lancet* 1: 391, 1970.

Draper, H. H., and Bell, R. R. Nutrition and osteoporosis. *Advances in Nutrition Research* 2: 79, 1979.

Ellis, F. R., et al. Incidence of osteoporosis in vegetarians and omnivores. *American Journal of Clinical Research* 25: 555, 1972.
Ettinger, B. Thyroid supplements: effect on bone mass. *Western Journal of Medicine* 136: 473, 1982.

Fruman, A. M., et al. Relationship of fasting urinary calcium to circulating estrogen and body weight in postmenopausal women. *Journal of Clinical Endocrinology and Metabolism* 50: 70, 1960.

Gallagher, J. C., et al. The crush fracture syndrome in post-menopausal women. *Clinics in Endocrinology and Metabolism* 2: 293, 1973.

Goldsmith, N. F., and Johnston, J. O. Bone mineral: Effects of oral contraceptives, pregnancy and lactation. *Journal of Bone and Joint Surgery* 57A: 657, 1975.

Gunson, D. E. Environmental zinc and cadmium pollution associated with generalized osteochrondrosis, osteoporosis and nephrocalcinosis in horses. *Journal of the American Veterinary Medicine Association* 180: 295, 1982.

Heaney, R. P., and Skillman, T. G. Calcium metabolism in normal human pregnancy. *Journal of Clinical Endocrinology and Metabolism* 33: 661, 1971.

Heaney, R. P., et al. Calcium balance and calcium requirements in middle-aged women. *American Journal of Clinical Nutrition* 30: 1603, 1979.

Heaney, R. P., et al. Menopausal changes in calcium balance performance. *Journal of Laboratory and Clinical Medicine* 92: 953, 1978.

Krawitt, E. L., Effect of acute ethanol administration on duodenal calcium transport. *Proceedings of the Society for Experimental Biology and Medicine* 146: 406, 1974.

Lanyon, L. E. Bone remodelling, mechanical stress and osteo-porosis. In *Osteoporosis. Recent advances in pathogenesis and treatment*, eds. H. F. DeLuca, et al. Baltimore, Maryland: University Park Press, 1981.

Lindquist, O., and Bengtsson, C. The effect of smoking on menopausal age. *Maturitas* 1: 171, 1979.

Lindsay, R. The influence of cigarette smoking on bone mass and bone loss. In *Osteoporosis. Recent advances in pathogenesis and treatment*, eds. H. F. DeLuca et al. Baltimore, Maryland: University Park Press, 1981.

Longcope, C., et al. Aromatization of androgens by muscle and adipose tissue in vivo. *Journal of Clinical Endocrinology and Metabolism* 46: 146, 1978.

McKenzie, L., and Notelovitz, M. Osteoporosis related fractures of the femur: The financial cost. Submitted for publication, 1982.

Marsh, A. G., et al. Cortical bone density of adult lacto-ovo-vegetarian and omnivorous women. *Journal of the American Dietetic Association* 76: 148, 1980.

Martinez-Maldonado, M., et al. Diuretics in nonedematous states. *Archives of Internal Medicine* 131: 797, 1978.

Matkovic, V., et al. Bone status and fracture rates in two regions of Yugoslavia. *American Journal of Clinical Nutrition* 32: 540, 1979.

Mazess, R. B., and Mather, W. Bone mineral content of North Alaskan Eskimos. *American Journal of Clinical Nutrition* 27: 916, 1974.

Nordin, B. E. C. International patterns of osteoporosis. *Clinical Orthopaedics and Related Research* 45: 17, 1966.

Nordin, B. E. C. Osteoporosis and calcium deficiency. In *Bone as a tissue*, ed. P. Fourman. New York: McGraw-Hill, 1960.

Porter, R. H., et al. Treatment of hypoparathyroid patients with chlorthalidone. *New England Journal of Medicine* 298: 577, 1978.

Smith, D. M., et al. Genetic factors in determining bone mass. *Journal of Clinical Investigation* 52: 2800, 1973.

Smith, R. W., and Rizek, J. Epidemiologic studies of osteoporosis in women of Puerto Rico and southeastern Michigan with reference to age, race, national origin and to other related or associated findings. *Clinical Orthopaedics and Related Research* 45: 31, 1966.

Spencer, H., and Lender, M. Adverse effects of aluminum-containing antacids on mineral metabolism. *Gastroenterology* 76: 603, 1979.

Trotter, M., et al. Densities of bones of white and negro skeletons. *Journal of Bone and Joint Surgery* 42A: 50, 1960.

Walker, A. R. P., et al. The influence of numerous pregnancies and lactations on bone dimensions in South African Bantu and Caucasian mothers. *Clinical Science* 42: 189, 1972.

Wallace, J. Ph.D. dissertation. Pennsylvania State University, University Park, 1982.

Chapter 5.   How to Tell If You Are Losing Bone

Albanese, A. A. *Bone loss: causes, detection and therapy.* New York: Alan R. Liss, 1977.

Albright, F., et al. Postmenopausal osteoporosis. *Journal of the American Medical Association* 116: 2465, 1941.

Cann, C. E., et al. Spinal mineral loss in oophorectomized women. *Journal of the American Medical Association* 244: 2056, 1980.

Cohn, S. H., ed. *Noninvasive measurements of bone mass and their clinical application.* Boca Raton, Florida: CRC Press, 1981.

Daniell, H. W. Osteoporosis of the slender smoker. Vertebral compression fractures and loss of metacarpal cortex in relation to postmenopausal cigarette smoking and lack of obesity. *Archives of Internal Medicine* 136: 298, 1976.

Lutwak, L., et al. Calcium deficiency and human periodontal disease. *Israel Journal of Medical Sciences* 7: 504, 1971.

McConkey, B., et al. Transparent skin and osteoporosis. *Lancet* 1: 693, 1963.

McConkey, B., et al. Transparent skin and osteoporosis. A study in patients with rheumatoid disease. *Annals of Rheumatic Diseases* 24: 219, 1965.

Reid, D. M., et al. Total body calcium in rheumatoid arthritis: Effects of disease activity and corticosteroid treatment. *British Medical Journal* 285: 330, 1982.

Chapter 6.   How to Prevent Osteoporosis

Daniell, H. W. Osteoporosis of the slender smoker. Vertebral compression fractures and loss of metacarpal cortex in relation to postmenopausal cigarette smoking and lack of obesity. *Archives of Internal Medicine* 136: 298, 1976.

High coffee intake intensifies calcium depletion after menopause. *Ob Gyn News,* May 1, 1982.

James, W., et al. Calcium binding by dietary fibre. *Lancet* 1: 638, 1978.

Johnson, N. E., et al. Effect of level of protein intake on urinary and fecal calcium and calcium retention of young adult males. *Journal of Nutrition* 100: 1423, 1970.

Kleeman, C. R., et al. Effect of variations in sodium intake on calcium excretion in normal humans. *Proceedings of the Society for Experimental Biology and Medicine* 115: 29, 1964.

Lutz, J., and Linkswiler, H. M. Calcium metabolism in post-menopausal and osteoporotic women consuming two levels of dietary protein. *American Journal of Clinical Nutrition* 34: 2178, 1981.

McCarron, D. A. Blood pressure: the balancing art. Paper presented at the 1981 National Dairy Council Food Writers Conference. New Orleans, Louisiana, and Nogales, Arizona.

McCarron, D. A. Low serum concentrations of ionized calcium in patients with hypertension. *New England Journal of Medicine* 307: 226, 1982.

McCarron, D. A., et al. Dietary calcium profiles in normal and hypertensive humans. *Clinical Research* 29: 267A 1981.

Malm, O. J. Calcium requirement and adaptation in adult men. Oslo: Oslo University Press, 1958.

Newcomer, A. D., et al. Lactase deficiency: prevalence in osteoporosis. *Annals of Internal Medicine* 89: 218, 1978.

Nordin, B. E. C. Clinical significance and pathogenesis of osteoporosis. *British Medical Journal* 1: 571, 1971.

Premature bone loss found in some nonmenstruating sportswomen (Medical News. Reported by Elizabeth Rasche Gonzalez.) *Journal of the American Medical Association* 248: 513, 1982.

Chapter 7.   Pros and Cons of Estrogen Therapy

Aitken, J. M., et al. Oestrogen replacement therapy for prevention of osteoporosis after oophorectomy. *British Medical Journal* 3: 515, 1973.

Christiansen, C., et al. Prevention of early postmenopausal bone loss: controlled 2-year study in 315 normal females. *European Journal of Clinical Investigation* 10: 273, 1980.

Gambrell, R. D., et al. Estrogen therapy and breast cancer in postmenopausal women. *Journal of the American Geriatrics Society* 28: 251, 1980.

Gambrell, R. D., et al. Reduced incidence of endometrial cancer among postmenopausal women treated with progestogens. *Journal of the American Geriatrics Society* 27: 389, 1979.

Geola, F. L., et al. Biological effects of various doses of conjugated equine estrogens in postmenopausal women. *Journal of Clinical Endocrinology and Metabolism* 51: 620, 1980.

Gordan, G. S., et al. Antifracture efficacy of long-term estrogens for osteoporosis. *Transactions of the Association of American Physicians* 86: 326, 1973.

Horsman, A., et al. Prospective trial of oestrogen and calcium in postmenopausal women. *British Medical Journal* 2: 789, 1977.

Hulka, B. S., et al. Breast cancer and estrogen replacement therapy. *American Journal of Obstetrics and Gynecology* 143: 638, 1982.

Hutchinson, T. A., et al. Post-menopausal oestrogens protect against fractures of hip and distal radius. *Lancet* 2: 705, 1979.

Lindsay, R., et al. Bone response to termination of oestrogen treatment. *Lancet* 1: 1325, 1978.

Lindsay, R., et al. Comparative effects of oestrogen and a progestogen on bone mass in postmenopausal women. *Clinical Science and Molecular Medicine* 54: 193, 1978.

Lindsay, R., et al. Long-term prevention of postmenopausal osteoporosis by oestrogen. *Lancet* 1: 1038, 1976.

Lindsay, R., et al. Prevention of spinal osteoporosis in oophorectomized women. *Lancet* 2: 1151, 1980.

Meema, H. E., and Meema, S. Prevention of postmenopausal osteoporosis by hormone treatment of the menopause. *Canadian Medical Association Journal* 99: 248, 1968.

Meema, S., et al. Preventive effect of estrogen on postmenopausal bone loss. *Archives of Internal Medicine* 135: 1436, 1975.

Nachtigall, L. E., et al. Estrogen replacement therapy. A 10-year prospective study in the relationship to osteoporosis. *Obstetrics and Gynecology* 53: 277, 1979.

Nordin, B. E. C., et al. Treatment of spinal osteoporosis in postmenopausal women. *British Medical Journal* 280: 451, 1980.

Recker, R. R., et al. Effect of estrogens and calcium carbonate on bone loss in postmenopausal women. *Annals of Internal Medicine* 87: 649, 1977.

Salmi, T. Risk factors in endometrial carcinoma. *Acta Obstetricia et Gynecologica Scandinavica.* Supplement 86, 1979.

Weiss, N. S., et al. Decreased risk of fractures of the hip and lower forearm with postmenopausal use of estrogen. *New England Journal of Medicine* 303: 1195, 1980.

Chapter 8.   If You Already Have Osteoporosis

Chesnut, C. H., et al. Assessment of anabolic steroids and calcitonin in the treatment of osteoporosis. In *Osteoporosis II*, ed. U. S. Barzel. New York: Grune & Stratton, 1979.

Chesnut, C. H., et al. Effect of methandrostenolone on post-menopausal bone wasting as assessed by changes in total bone mineral mass. *Metabolism* 26: 267, 1977.

Jungreis, S. W., Personal communication, March 1, 1982. Medical Research Center, Brookhaven National Laboratory, Upton, New York.

Lane, J. Postmenopausal osteoporosis: the orthopedic approach. *The Female Patient* 6: 43, 1981.

Riggs, B. L., et al. Effect of the fluoride/calcium regimen on vertebral fracture occurrence in postmenopausal osteoporosis. Comparison with conventional therapy. *New England Journal of Medicine* 306: 446, 1982.

Chapter 9. How to Help Your Daughter Prevent Osteoporosis

Minton, S. D., et al. Bone mineral content in term and preterm appropriate-for-gestational-age infants. *Journal of Pediatrics* 95: 1037, 1979.

Recker, R. R. Continuous treatment of osteoporosis: current status. *Orthopedic Clinics of North America* 12: 611, 1981.

CREDITS

Page 62: Hip Fracture Rate in Yugoslavian Women with High and Low Calcium Diets. Matkovic, V., et al. *American Journal of Clinical Nutrition* 32:540, 1979.

Page 63: Calcium Needs and Intake with Age. Albanese, A. A., et al. *Calcium Throughout the Life Cycle*. National Dairy Council, 1978.

Page 96: Calcium Equivalent Chart. Albanese, A. A., et al. *Calcium Throughout the Life Cycle*. National Dairy Council, 1978.

Page 116: Prevention of Bone Loss After Menopause with Estrogen Therapy. Lindsay, R., et al. *Lancet* 1:1038, 1974.

Page 116: Discontinued Estrogen Treatment. Lindsay, R., et al. *Lancet* 1:1325, 1978.

Page 121: Prevention of Bone Loss with Estrogen-Progesterone Therapy: Christiansen, C., et al. *European Journal of Clinical Investigation* 10:273, 1980.

Page 27: Bone Loss with Age: A Comparison of Men and Women. Riggs, B. L., et al. *Journal of Clinical Investigation* 67:328, 1981.

Page 36: Wrist Fractures in Men and Women. Knowelden, J., et al. *British Journal of Preventive and Social Medicine*. 18:130, 1974.

Page 129: Back Exercises. Lane, J. *The Female Patient* 6:43, 1981.

Index

A

Calcium Diary

For seven consecutive days, you should record everything you eat and drink. This includes all snacks between meals! Don't forget to include calcium supplements if you are taking them, as well as any vitamin or mineral supplements. To determine if you have excessive amounts of the "bone robbers," keep track of them as well.

CALCIUM DIARY
MONDAY

Type and amount of food, drink	Amount of calcium (milligrams)
BREAKFAST	
LUNCH	
DINNER	
SNACKS	

Vitamin and mineral supplements:

"Bone robbers" (include alcohol, smoking, coffee):

Did you exercise today?

CALCIUM DIARY
TUESDAY

	Type and amount of food, drink	Amount of calcium (milligrams)
BREAKFAST		
LUNCH		
DINNER		
SNACKS		

Vitamin and mineral supplements:

"Bone robbers" (include alcohol, smoking, coffee):

Did you exercise today?

CALCIUM DIARY
WEDNESDAY

	Type and amount of food, drink	Amount of calcium (milligrams)
BREAKFAST		
LUNCH		
DINNER		
SNACKS		

Vitamin and mineral supplements:

"Bone robbers" (include alcohol, smoking, coffee):

Did you exercise today?

CALCIUM DIARY
THURSDAY

	Type and amount of food, drink	Amount of calcium (milligrams)
BREAKFAST		
LUNCH		
DINNER		
SNACKS		

Vitamin and mineral supplements:

"Bone robbers" (include alcohol, smoking, coffee):

Did you exercise today?

CALCIUM DIARY
FRIDAY

	Type and amount of food, drink	Amount of calcium (milligrams)
BREAKFAST		
LUNCH		
DINNER		
SNACKS		

Vitamin and mineral supplements:

"Bone robbers" (include alcohol, smoking, coffee):

Did you exercise today?

CALCIUM DIARY
SATURDAY

	Type and amount of food, drink	Amount of calcium (milligrams)
BREAKFAST		
LUNCH		
DINNER		
SNACKS		

Vitamin and mineral supplements:

"Bone robbers" (include alcohol, smoking, coffee):

Did you exercise today?

CALCIUM DIARY
SUNDAY

	Type and amount of food, drink	Amount of calcium (milligrams)
BREAKFAST		
LUNCH		
DINNER		
SNACKS		

Vitamin and mineral supplements:

"Bone robbers" (include alcohol, smoking, coffee):

Did you exercise today?

Osteoporosis:
A Syndrome Of Twos

All the presented information may seem confusing and overwhelming at first, but osteoporosis is really quite an easy process to understand. It can be best summarized as a syndrome of twos:

* There are two types of bone involved:
    Cortical — the hard bone of your arms and legs
    Trabecular — the spongy bone of your vertebrae

* Bone growth and bone loss are dependent upon the activity of two types of cells:
    Osteoclasts — the bone-removing cells
    Osteoblasts — the bone-building cells

* There are two rates of normal bone loss:
    Early — trabecular bone loss, which begins in the 20s
    Later — cortical bone loss, which begins in the 30s and accelerates after menopause.

* There are two degrees of increased bone loss:
    Osteopenia — less bone than normal, but still enough not to fracture.
    Osteoporosis — much less bone than normal, leading to fractures.

* Osteoporosis is likely to develop if a woman:
    Reaches bone maturity with decreased bone mass.
    Loses bone at too rapid a rate (faster than 1% per year).

* There are two clinical types of osteoporosis:

Trabecular — characterized by loss of height, spinal curvature, and vertebral fractures.

Cortical — characterized by fractures of the wrist or hip.

* There are two classifications of osteoporosis:

Primary — usually due to a single identifiable cause, such as a drug or disease.

Secondary — a multifactorial disorder involving genetic, nutritional, exercise, and environmental factors.

* There are two methods of diagnosing osteoporosis:

Indirectly — by measuring loss of height or changes in the blood or urine.

Directly — by measuring changes in the density of bones.

* There are two clinical presentations of osteoporosis:

Asymptomatic — no obvious fracture or deformity. (Osteoporosis and subsequent fractures are preventable at this point.)

Symptomatic — fracturing has already occurred. (Treatment is directed toward preventing further bone loss and fractures.)

* There are two treatment principles for osteoporosis.

Nonspecific — includes nutritional and exercise strategies.

Specific — includes correcting the cause of bone loss if known and treatment with hormones or one of the new, experimental treatments.